D0593297

uncl
c686

Yours Sincerely
Wm S Bigelow

THE BIBLE
THAT WAS LOST
AND IS FOUND

By

JOHN BIGELOW

" . . . I hope in thy word."
"Uphold me according unto thy word, that I may live:
  and let me not be ashamed of my hope."
"I am thy servant; give me understanding, that I may
  know thy testimonies."

Psalm cxix, 81, 116, 125.

✠

NEW YORK
NEW-CHURCH BOARD OF PUBLICATION
1912

231
B481b

BX
8711
B5

Copyright, 1912, by
New-Church Board of Publication.

U.M.C. Duplicates Room

1-M-63

C686

18806

INTRODUCTION.

While John Bigelow was yet visibly among us, he was frequently besought to give wider publicity to the account which he prepared for the inner circle of his family and spiritual companions of how he came to have such an abiding faith in Emanuel Swedenborg as a divinely commissioned interpreter of the Sacred Scriptures and a revelator of truths of angelic wisdom. Those of us who were privileged to know him well, and who loved to hear him converse on spiritual themes, know that he treasured this part of his life's experiences as something that was peculiarly sacred. Implicit as was his faith, unbounded as was his enthusiasm, there never was the slightest trace of self-confidence or pride of intelligence. Firm in his belief, he was never dogmatic. He was unflinchingly loyal to the system of truth to which he felt he owed so much of his life's happiness, but he was extremely catholic. The spirit of sectarianism was not in him. He longed, rather, to see the truths which had made the Word of God a veritable lamp to his feet and a light to his path available to all who might profit by them, irrespective of any claims of denominationalism. He found satisfaction in going Sunday after Sunday to the Church on East Thirty-fifth street; and, while he never faltered in his attachment to it, truth compels me to say that his interest and his hopes were never confined to the local organization which prized his spiritual fellowship, and for which he did so much.

It was in the spring of 1911 that I went to Mr. Bigelow and asked him, for the sake of the good that might be accomplished, to allow me to edit this present volume. I urged that at the time when the tercentenary of the Authorized Version of our English Bible was being celebrated, it was peculiarly fitting that he should make public his testimony as to how the Bible had been established for him as the veritable Word of God. He listened to me patiently as I tried to persuade him that the narration of his religious experiences might be helpful to many outside of his own immediate circle of friends. He was unfeignedly modest on this point, but he promised to consider the matter. A few days later he wrote that he felt he had no right to withhold anything that might prove useful, and that he would leave the matter entirely in my hands. He sent me a copy of his "Bible That Was Lost and Is Found," in which he had indicated changes and additions that should be made, and with it a large number of letters from friends who had received copies of the original edition. In his characteristic way he said that he felt I was entitled to any assistance he could place at my disposal, inasmuch as I was willing to act as a midwife in the birth of this new progeny.

A little later, at a time when he felt that the last hours of his earthly life were drawing to a close, he dictated the following lines:

"I am very ill. It is doubtful whether I shall ever see you again in this world, or live to see the little book you have so kindly volunteered

2

to mother. It is a satisfaction to me to reflect that, before I am called away, I am permitted to make a contribution to the Christian Church which you think may prove useful to the world I am soon to leave behind me. I am too feeble to say anything more, except to invoke the blessing of our Father in heaven upon * * * the modest Church with which we both have so many glorious associations."

It could not be otherwise than that in preparing this book to go forth on what I confidently expect to be a mission of wide usefulness, I have counted it a labor of love; a labor of love to one of the grandest of men, whom the Lord in His good Providence has raised up to be so worthy a witness of the truths of His New Church.

JULIAN K. SMYTH.

New York City,
June, 1912.

PREFACE TO THE FIRST EDITION.

My Dear Children:

When Joshua was about to cross the Jordan with the Ark of the Covenant to enter the Promised Land, he was commanded by the Lord to select one man from each tribe to take charge of the ark who, "out of the midst of Jordan where the Priests' feet stood firm," were "to take twelve stones; carry them over with them, and lay them down in the lodging place where they should lodge that night." Joshua complied with these instructions, and when the people came up out of Jordan, the Lord said to them, "When your children shall ask their fathers in time to come saying, What mean these stones? then ye shall let your children know, saying, 'Israel came over this Jordan on dry land. For the Lord your God dried up the waters of Jordan from before you until ye were passed over, as the Lord your God did to the Red Sea which He dried up from before us until we were passed over; that all the people of the earth may know the hand of the Lord that it is mighty, that they may fear the Lord your God forever.' "

The duty here imposed by the Lord upon Joshua and his followers to commemorate the passage of Israel in safety through the Red Sea and over Jordan, was not a duty imposed merely to meet a temporary exigency of

5

a transient population, but like all duties imposed by Jehovah-Lord was of universal application, and as enduring as Truth and Right; and every person who has the grace to realize that he has been led by the same mighty hand and outstretched arm safely out of the bondage of false doctrines and through a wilderness beset with temptations and peril, into the freedom of those whom the Truth makes free, is bound to testify by some equally unequivocal memorial a grateful sense of his deliverance.

Under the inspiration of this sacred lesson, and in the humble hope of rendering my experience possibly of use to you and perhaps to some others, I have prepared the following narrative of the circumstances which led to my own deliverance from a spiritual bondage no less oppressive and degrading, nor, I imagine, very different from that which the Israelites endured in Egypt. I hope that with God's blessing it may help you to remember the Red Sea and the Jordan which every regenerating soul must cross, and encourage you on the journey to put your trust absolutely and exclusively in the guidance and protection of Him who never leaves a prayer unanswered; who never refuses an appeal to Him but in mercy, and who never neglects an opportunity of promoting the welfare of any of His creatures.

YOUR AFFECTIONATE FATHER.

21 *Gramercy Park,*
New York, Christmas, 1893.

6

PREFACE TO THE SECOND EDITION.

The narrative which is here, and now for the first time submitted to the public, was prepared and privately printed some years ago for the information of my children and a few friends who, for personal reasons, were likely to take an interest in its revelations. From most of the latter, and among them were many whose judgment was entitled to great weight with me, I received earnest appeals to give it to the public. I shrank, however, from incurring even a suspicion of attaching undue importance to experiences and opinions of such a strictly personal character, or of presuming to commend them specially to the consideration of an exoteric circle. Since then times have changed, and I have changed with them. I have allowed myself to be persuaded that the time has arrived in the ecclesiastical evolution of our own country at least, when it is not impossible nor even improbable that there are many who may find deliverance from baleful doubts or pernicious illusions, and have an impaired faith in the Bible strengthened by the process to which I feel myself to be supremely indebted and which I have attempted in these pages to describe.

The Christian Church rests at every point for its foundations upon the Divine authorship and inspiration of at least the greater part of what is known as the

7

Holy Bible. To displace one stone of that foundation is thought by many, and I think correctly, to convert the Christian Church into a group of quasi religious clubs having only secular charters, and with no better guaranty for endurance than a Bank or an Insurance Corporation. Between the labors of the Scientists outside the Church, and the Critical miners inside the Church, teachings that would have imperilled the liberty if not the lives of their authors a century or two ago, are not only publicly taught from pulpits and professional chairs, but are sanctioned by the most highly accredited ecclesiastical organizations in our land. The Bible is dealt with by scholars of influence and distinction as literature merely, and judged by them in the same literary spirit as they would judge the Sentences of Marcus Antoninus. From one Episcopal pulpit we were recently told that "it is probably true that ninety per cent. of our bishops believe and teach views for which Bishop Colenso was deposed." Another speaks of the New Testament as "a bundle of left-over documents." Still another insists that the first two chapters of Matthew form simply a beautiful legend.

Even in the face of these painful disclosures, I hope it is with becoming diffidence that I venture to dissent from those who quarrel with what it is the fashion to call "Higher Criticism," and who denounce it as, "Evil and for evil only good." I cannot believe that more harm can come from the study of God's Word than from the study of His works.

We are all united in encouraging the application of Higher Criticism to the stars, to the garb of the earth and the treasures concealed in its bowels; we erect monuments in honor of the men who correct our erroneous impressions of any of Nature's laws; why should we honor the critical student of God's Word less than the critical student of His works, if both are working with an equal singleness of eye to the truth?

Nor will I disguise my conviction, without in the least undervaluing the work of the Christian Pulpit, that it has accomplished far less than has the Higher Criticism during the last century by stimulating throughout the world an inclination "to search the Scriptures," and rallying the nobler energies of humanity to their defence. Accustomed as most Christians are to listen to ministers and associate with people who take the Divine origin of the Bible for granted, we grow up knowing little or nothing about its everlasting foundations. It is only when they are assailed that earnest Christians set to work to investigate the imputed weakness of those foundations, and are thus equipped to demonstrate their impregnability.

It was in the Wilderness, according to the prophet Isaiah, that the way of the Lord was to be prepared and made straight; and "a highway for our God" in the desert.

So, false ideas, superannuated dogmas, sectarian prejudices must be overcome and exterminated before we are prepared for the unconditional reception of new truths.

To abandon a class of opinions and replace them with one of opposite opinions involves our being for a time— for a moment at least—without either; when our minds are vastated, a desert without grass or herb yielding seed. Our condition may be compared to that of a man

9

on the top of a mountain having occasion to cross to the top of an opposite mountain. He must descend to the valley that separates these mountains before he can begin to ascend the mountain opposite. So we must descend the mountain of fallacious dogma to the valley of absolute unbelief, before we can ascend the Holy Mountain of Divine Truth. Hence it rarely, if ever, happens that a person changes what he calls his religion without becoming, for a time at least, an agnostic or an unbeliever. The Israelites were required to wander forty years in the Wilderness before they could be cured of their polytheistic delusions and made to believe that there was but one God and He the Maker of Heaven and Earth, without whom was nothing made that was made.

Only our Heavenly Father knows whether at the last, Peter or Thomas would have made the greater sacrifices for his Lord and Master.

Perhaps one of the greatest troubles with which the visible Church on earth has had to contend, has been the fact that its members have not searched the Scriptures, that they have perused them too commonly with the eyes only, and like the penitent counting her beads, as a pious ceremonial, rather than with any expectation of drawing from that affluent fountain, "living water of which, whosoever drinketh shall never thirst." If the Bible be the Word of God, it is necessarily infinite truth. It can be nothing else. No finite being can therefore hope to understand all that it expresses. No book of which finite man could comprehend all or any part of the contents entirely, could possibly be the Word of God. We learn the lessons of God's Word as we learn those which are taught by His works, which constitute our earthly or natural environment, little by little; and yet the navigator of the ocean of Natural Science finds its shores recede from him as fast if not faster than he approaches them. So it will ever be. The truths of God's Word must also and always be mastered little by little, and only so far and so fast as we qualify ourselves to receive and assimilate them in our lives. We can never know absolute truth, but we can always be increasing our knowledge of what seems to us truth, and which therefore is to us ethically true. While we can never expect to understand all the wisdom of God's Word, whether recorded in the Bible or in nature, we can always be growing more and more into His image by studying both. Anything therefore that concentrates attention upon God's Word and invites or provokes men to the study of it, enlarges the sphere of its influence. The only faithful student of the Bible is the critical student, he who searches to find its hidden meaning. But he will at no time find in it so much of what seems to him to be truth, that his estimate of it may not be greatly modified by subsequent perusals. Unless the Bible seems like a new book every time it is read, no matter how frequently, it is because it has not been read thoughtfully, reverently, indeed I may say, critically. All the lessons of the Bible can no more be apprehended from a single perusal than the productive power of a farm can be harvested in a single crop. There is nothing more fatal to the diffusion of spiritual truth than using the Word like a chaplet or leaving it in too costly binding for use as a profession of faith on the parlor table. The eloquent Bishop of New York improved a recent occasion to probe this evil in an official communication, in the course of which he said:

"A modern fetichism which has dishonored the Bible by claiming to be its elect guardian, has shut it up these many years within the iron walls of a *dreary literalism,* robbing it thus alike of interest and of power."

Criticism even in a hostile spirit has never succeeded in seriously obstructing the diffusion of God's truth or the coming of His kingdom on the earth. The Bible has been no end of times like Jesus of Nazareth, dragged to the brow of a hill to be cast down from it; but like Jesus, it has always passed through the midst of its enemies, and gone on its way in every such crisis giving new and more impressive evidence of its Divine mission.

Voltaire's presumptuous boast that he had given the Christian Church its *coup de grâce* provoked the synchronous establishment of the British Bible Society which has spread the sacred record throughout the world in every written tongue, and among millions who had never heard either of it or of its divine author. When the learned Bishop of New York proclaimed that a modern fetichism which has dishonored the Bible by claiming to be its elect guardian, had *shut it up through many years within the iron walls of a dreary literalism,* he administered a more serious and wide reaching rebuke to the bishops and other clergy of his Church than had ever before emanated from the Episcopal bench in our time. And he uttered a truth, too, which promises to mark an epoch in the evolution of Bible religion. It has brought the religious communion of which he is the hierarchical head in his diocese face to face with several questions of considerable gravity.

Here are some of them:

1. What does his Reverence mean by the word "literalism," whether dreary or otherwise, that has made the Bible for many years the victim of a modern fetichism; does he mean that the Bible is not literally true, and therefore to that extent at least not inspired?

2. Must not any book which is not literally true, be to the same extent literally untrue, and so far misleading?

3. If true in any sense, how is that sense to be ascertained?

4. Does the Bishop propose to let his Church mark time while Dr. Briggs and other critical students find out the portions of the Bible which are inspired, if any, and those which are not; or would he restrict the reading of the entire Bible to a class set apart and trained to select the portions suitable for the flock, as the Latin Church has done?

5. What tribunal have we that is competent to guarantee the superiority of the Canon of Dr. Briggs, to that of St. Jerome?

To all these questions is there any answer which would not be fatal to any pretensions of the Bible to be regarded as the Word of God or as a Rule of Faith to men, that is, better than that which was embodied in the words of Paul when writing on behalf of himself and his companions to the Romans, he said that now "We serve in the newness of the spirit and not in the oldness of the letter"?

13

Let it be observed that Paul notices the oldness of the letter, but seems to have had no notion of its dreariness. What he meant by oldness here may be inferred from what he said in his famous 13th Chapter of his first Epistle to the Corinthians, "When I was a child I spake as a child, I felt as a child, I thought as a child: now that I am become a man, I put away childish things. For now we see through a glass darkly [the letter of the law] but then [when that which is perfect is come] face to face: now I know in part, but then shall I know even as also I have been known."

This comparison of the thoughts and feelings of the childish mind with those of the adult, expresses to my mind the precise distinction between the uses of the literal garb of the Bible and of its spiritual contents. Paul does not pretend to undervalue what he felt, thought or did as a child. He merely calls attention to the difference between the natural and the spiritual intelligence, the one enlightened by love, and the other not, or only partially, so enlightened.

Here I am prompted to ask whether the Bible may not be true to some in one sense and to others in another sense? No book is true to a child in the sense that it is true to a grown person. In fact, science has never been able to teach us anything which did not expand or contract in its dimensions with increasing knowledge and experience. The world believed, no one knows how many thousand years, that the sun revolved around the earth, and the only Church, which claims dogmatically to be infallible, treated as a blasphemous heresy any denial of it. Even to this day we all speak of the sun's rising and setting, a statement scientifically absurd but perfectly true as understood by both speaker and hearer. The sun does rise and set to us, for such is the report of the fact as daily made to us by our senses.

When a ship leaves the port of San Francisco for Japan no one ever questions the report that she is sailing westward, and yet in point of fact she is moving with incalculable rapidity in precisely the opposite direction.

Æsop's fables of the wolf complaining of the lamb for polluting the stream at which both are drinking; of the grasshopper asking alms of the ant; of the competitive trial of the wind and the sun to compel the traveller to take off his cloak, are all as true as any history is to the child, but no less true to the adult though in a very different sense. Why may not the literal sense of the Bible be the repository of as much and as important truths to undeveloped and untutored minds, a class which would include by far the larger part of the human race, and at the same time to more developed minds teach a class of truths far more profound, but in no important sense inconsistent with them? No one would propose to prohibit the reading of Æsop's fables because he represented animals as talking a written language. There is little doubt that children absorb more important truths by the perusal of those fables according to their measure of intelligence than adults do, though not a single fact as stated in them is literally true.

To do precisely what Paul said he had done, is what the so-called orthodox Churches of our day have hitherto refused, or rather perhaps neglected, to do, but what they must do before they can emancipate the Bible from the "dreary literalism" in which it is immured.

Their clergy must be ministers of a new covenant; not of the letter, but of the spirit. To emphasize that necessity at a moment which seems specially propitious for its consideration, has been my only excuse for presuming to enlarge the circle for which the following narrative was originally prepared.

    The Squirrels
        June 7, 1911.

I

COULD I believe that any one event in our lives was more strictly Providential than another, I should say without hesitation that the event or series of events which led me to the island of St. Thomas in the winter of 1854 deserves that distinction. When I left home I had but one well defined purpose, aside from a little recreation; that was to visit Hayti to see what sort of work, Africans born and bred in slavery, were making of self-government, a question about which public sentiment in the United States was then seriously divided and in which both as a journalist and a patriot I then felt a special interest. I had no thought of going farther. I had no curiosity to see St. Thomas or any of its inhabitants. I was borne thither, too, by a chain of incidents, every one of which I would gladly have avoided. It proved to be the only way by which I could get home to the United States without indefinite delay. Port-au-Prince, where I had my headquarters while in Hayti, was desolated by yellow and other malignant fevers to such an extent that for four or five weeks of my stay there, most of the vessels in port were prevented from leaving for lack of sailors. Of the entire crew of the bark that brought me to Hayti, all but two were in the cemetery within four days after my arrival. Thus, when ready to return, I was compelled, to my serious inconvenience, to cross to St. Thomas in the hope of

17

there getting a steamer for New York. On my arrival at that island, however, I found that the New York steamer—there was then but one on the line—had met with an accident on her last homeward voyage; at least such was the information given out by her agents, and had gone into dock in New York for repairs, how long to be detained there, no one at St. Thomas professed to know. I afterward had reason to suspect that the accident, if any had been sustained, had been sufficiently magnified to make it serve as a pretext for withdrawing her temporarily from an unprofitable service, St. Thomas being at this time in a more distressed sanitary condition, even, than Hayti. A French emigrant ship, bound to some port in South America, had been driven in there in distress only a few days before my arrival, and compelled to discharge her cargo there. The negroes of the island who were employed for this work, were stimulated to unaccustomed fatigue and exposure under a broiling sun, by extra pay. After thus being overheated by day, they knew no better than to lay themselves down to sleep on their door mats as usual at night, without any covering and in most cases without a roof over them. The consequence in nearly every instance was a chill, for the temperature at midnight was from 40 to 50 degrees lower than at noon; and the cholera broke out on the very next day with such virulence that, within a month after the arrival of the distressed vessel, one-tenth of the population of the island were in their graves. This state of things necessarily prolonged my detention, for the vessels in the harbor by which I might have hoped to get to Havana or to some other Spanish port in steam communication with New York, could get no charters for any of the Spanish islands because of the rigorous and prolonged quarantine to which they were sure to be condemned for having sailed last from a cholera-infected district. Consequently I had no alternative but to take up my quarters at the principal, indeed the only hotel on the island,—by no means a bad one,—kept by a Creole Spaniard who had formerly conducted a similar business at the city of St. Domingo, and there await the slow revolution of the wheel of fortune.

The only guest sleeping in the hotel—though a number of residents took their meals there—was a Danish lawyer by the name of Kjerulff, who had practised his profession for many years in St. Thomas, but like myself, was temporarily established at the hotel, awaiting an opportunity of getting to the United States where he had some pecuniary interests which he seemed disposed to increase. We naturally fell into a sort of acquaintance that commonly follows contiguity, and which ripened rapidly when he discovered that we had some common difficulties to overcome and a common destination.

One morning during the second week of my sojourn on the island, Mr. Kjerulff and I chanced both to be seated in the spacious, but then deserted dining hall—deserted by every one but ourselves, I mean—he at one end and I at the other, and both with books in our hands. I was reading the Bible.

II

It is necessary for me here to premise that both my parents were Presbyterians by inheritance and conviction, and I was brought up according to the straitest of the sect. In my eleventh year, however, I was sent to boarding school, and it was never my privilege to live at home again with my parents except in my school and professional vacations. As a consequence, I suppose, of being thus thrown very much upon my own resources, I early in life fell or rose, I cannot say which, into the habit of judging for myself, according to my limited lights, of the logical and theological merits of what I heard from the pulpit and read in the Bible. I began quite early to discern what looked to me like inconsistencies and improbabilities in its pages. Their number multiplied with my growth, and all the faster from the fact that my spiritual guides, for the most part, failed to impress me as men of strong convictions, or as having a particular call to break the bread of life to hungering souls. Bad logic and sectarian sophisms in the pulpit have unquestionably a tendency to encourage a propensity to question the truth of everything that comes from the same fountain. They certainly had that effect upon me. Besides, young men always experience more or less satisfaction in detecting what they suppose to be the errors of those who aspire to be thought wiser or better than themselves. So, between vanity and honest doubt, I fear I had been spending more time in looking up what I considered inconsistencies in the Word than in searching for what might have been useful in forming my character and in directing my daily walk and conversation. With the light which the pulpit offered me in those days, I did not see how God could have loved His only-begotten Son less than the world, which was under His condemnation for its sins; nor how the wicked could be any better fitted for heaven by the death of any one, and especially of an innocent person; nor how God could derive any satisfaction from the suffering of His innocent offspring; nor, if Christ's death was a satisfaction for the sins of the world, why any sinner, after His expiatory death, should suffer or be called to account for any sins subsequently committed, His redemption having been duly purchased and paid for; nor was it at all clear to me how Christ's death could be the infinite sacrifice it was represented to be, when He knew He was to rise again three days after His crucifixion and resume His seat on the right hand of the Father. I was accustomed from my earliest youth to repeat the prayer recommended by our Lord as a model to His disciples, in which the Father is asked to lead us not into temptation. When I came to read in James that "God cannot be tempted with evil, nor tempteth He any man," I was puzzled to comprehend the propriety of this invocation, which virtually reproached God with doing what James gives us to understand it would be sinful even to suspect Him of doing.

The Mosaic Cosmogony also bristled with difficulties. I tried in vain to reconcile the indisputable fact that the sun is the source of all light on our planet, with the record in Genesis that the creation of light was the work of the first day of creation, vegetables of the third, while the sun, without which there obviously could have been neither light nor vegetation, was not created until the fourth day. And how could the days have mornings and evenings, as they are reported to have had, before the sun was created? And when I found the champions of the Bible pretending to have reconciled the 6,000-year-old theory of creation with the teachings of geology, by maintaining that the "days" of creation, as given by Moses, meant not a day of twenty-four hours, but an indefinite period of time—hundreds, thousands, millions of years—I not unnaturally inferred that they had taken refuge in a greater absurdity than the one they sought to avoid, for the seventh day on which "God rested from all his work which he had made," must have been as long as either of the days which preceded it.

This taste for hunting and running down what seemed to me incongruous, inconsistent or inconsequential passages of the letter of the Word grew by what it fed on, and it is mortifying and painful for me now to think how blind and stupid I was all this time, while flattering myself that I was profitably employed.

About 1842, and soon after my admission to the bar, circumstances threw me into more or less intimate relations with a lawyer, who had won for himself considerable reputation as a barrister. He subsequently held one of the highest judicial positions in the State. He was twelve or fourteen years my senior; he took a fancy to me for reasons I do not yet quite understand; perhaps because I always had a rather uncommon capacity for tolerating the eccentricities and peculiarities of others, for we had very little in common. I respected his talents and manly character, I enjoyed his conversation, which though somewhat critical, not to say censorious, was always sparkling, and usually instructive, at least to one who was so much his junior. We had lodgings under the same roof and took our meals at the same hotels for many years and until he married, when I served as one of his groomsmen. Before coming to New York to reside he had been captivated by the teachings then novel of Gall and Spurzheim, and had been one of several gentlemen who united in inviting Dr. Combe, of Edinburgh, to come to the United States to expound their new science. He adopted the views of this school of philosophers unreservedly, and by degrees he drifted so far toward fatalism as to deny moral accountability, rather than admit that a man's cranial developments, rather than his will, were not binding upon, or determinative of, his conduct and character. He had not been brought up by his parents to entertain any reverence for the Bible or respect for the Church or clergy, and when my acquaintance with him began, he was accustomed to speak of the sacred volume as the "razor strop," that being, according to his view, and the view of many of his early friends, the most useful purpose to which they had seen it applied. Though destitute of any particle of reverence for the Word, and though he rarely put his foot inside of a Church, he was notably conscientious. The ethical side of his character was as fully developed on the natural plane as in any person I had then ever met. In judging men or conduct, he habitually looked to ethical though not spiritual conditions as the decisive ones. He was a fine, often an eloquent talker, and his spectroscopic methods of analyzing the motives of human conduct were new to me then, and in some respects extremely profitable. Unhappily, with them he did much to quicken into new life, suspicions that had been slowly germinating in my mind,

23

that what I failed to comprehend in the Bible was a defect in it instead of in myself.

This suspicion gained upon me as time rolled on, though the devastation of the religious notions in which I had been trained was not rapid. I could not name any particular event, or any particular time, from which my faith in the Revealed Religion began consciously to weaken; nor when in my spiritual horizon the sun actually stood still upon Gibeon and the moon in the Valley of Ajalon. I drifted with a current, the force and direction of which never attracted my attention nor occupied my thoughts till I found myself approaching the open sea of disbelief.

At the time of my visit to St. Thomas I suppose I had pretty much ceased to regard the Bible as possessing any higher sanction than the writings of Marcus Aurelius or of Confucius, except that it taught a loftier and more comprehensive system of morals. Jesus of Nazareth I regarded as one of the best of men, if such a man ever existed, of which I was not at all clear; but the method of His incarnation, His miracles and resurrection, I sometimes doubted. I inclined to class them with the stories of Hercules and Theseus. I did not hesitate to ask myself, "Is not this the carpenter, the son of Mary, the brother of James and of Judah and Simon?" If I attended any Church, it was usually that of Dr. Follen or Dr. Dewey, who then occupied the only two Unitarian pulpits in the city, where I repaired for literary rather than for spiritual refreshment.

The Old Testament I regarded, at least I thought I regarded, pretty much as Cobden once told me that he regarded it, as a book written for the Jews only, but not for us. I say I thought I so regarded it, but I have since doubted whether I really thought much about it; and whether these doubts of the divine origin of the Word were not mere surface indications, manifesting themselves during a period of rapid physical and mental growth, while the wiser lessons and training of my early youth were hibernating in the heart in a state of temporary torpidity; for even in those days I could never treat my Bible with neglect or disrespect, nor could I hear it spoken of in a profane way without an unpleasant sensation. Why I had this feeling or whence it came, I had then no suspicion, and, perhaps, if provoked to explain or defend it, like Peter I should have disowned it. I dare say that in this respect my experience is not uncommon. Bunyan, in his "Grace Abounding," reports a somewhat similar confirmation of the old proverb that the horse that drags its halter is not lost. "This I well remember," he says, "that though I could myself sin with the greatest delight and ease, and also take pleasure in the violence of my companions; yet, even then, if I had at any time seen wicked things in those who professed goodness, it would make my spirit tremble. And once above all the rest, when I was in the height of vanity, yet hearing one swear that was reported for a religious man, it had so great a shock upon my spirit that it made my heart ache."

With all my critical difficulties I still found the Bible about the most interesting book in my library, nor had I any other book to which I so frequently turned for entertainment, even after I had ceased to turn to it for any better purpose. As Herod feared John, knowing that he was just and holy, and heard him gladly, so I

25

must have feared the Word, knowing that it was just and so far holy, and, despite my Pyrrhonism, I read it, though perhaps with only a pagan's interest.

III

WE will now return to the dining hall of the hotel of St. Thomas. I have said that I was reading the Bible. I had read everything readable that I had brought with me from home, and had bought and read everything readable in the solitary bookstore at St. Thomas. In fact I had procured from it a copy of Macaulay's History of England then fresh from the London press, and which, in my then starving condition, I had greedily devoured. I had done the island thoroughly, and my Bible was all that was left upon which to expend my superfluity of leisure. It so happened that I was reading the 12th chapter of Genesis, which gives the account of Abram driven by a famine into Egypt. When I had finished it I said to Mr. Kjerulff, "Is it not extraordinary that this book should be accepted by the most highly civilized nations of the earth as the Word of God? Just listen." I then read the verses, with which the chapter to which I have referred concludes, in which the patriarch passes off Sarah his wife for his sister.

"This Abram," said I, "is the man whom it is pretended our Father in Heaven had selected from all the people of the earth as most deserving of His favour; had promised to make of him a great nation; to bless him; to bless them that bless him; to curse them that curse him, and that in him all the families of the earth should be blessed. And yet almost the first thing we

26

hear of him is his commanding his wife to tell a falsehood, which inevitably exposed her to insult and de-
gradation, apparently for the sole purpose of saving
himself from apprehended, but, as the event proved,
imaginary dangers. Does not the Egyptian," I asked,
"whom the Bible represents as the oppressor of God's
people, appear, according to our standards at least, to
have been the better man of the two?"

"Well, yes," replied Mr. Kjerulff, "it does appear so
at first."

"But," said I, "does it not appear so all the time?"

Mr. Kjerulff seemed rather to avoid a direct answer
to my question, and in turn asked me if I had ever read
any of the writings of Swedenborg. I said that I could
not say that I had, that a friend had once lent me a
treatise on "Conjugal Love" when I was a law student,
but I then considered my friend* something of a crank,
and his recommendation of a book, therefore, did not
help it much to my favor; besides, I was not at the time
interested, nor possibly capable of being interested, in
the subject of which it treated, so that I had no recollec-
tion of anything I read in it, which at most could not
have been much. "Well," said Mr. Kjerulff, "in his
Arcana Cœlestia, Swedenborg has given an exposition
of the chapter you have been reading, which, perhaps,
would satisfy you that there is more in it than you seem
to suspect." I intimated mildly that there was no ob-
scurity about the meaning, and that I did not see how
any one could get any impression of those verses dif-

* This was Dr. Hemphill, a learned young German, who subsequently became a physician of the Homœopathic School and
author of some valuable works on Homœopathic Science.

27

ferent from mine. Mr. Kjerulff then went on to explain something about an interior meaning and spiritual correspondence, etc. Failing entirely to understand what he was talking about, I asked him if he had the work to which he referred. He said he had it somewhere, but he was not sure that he had it with him in his luggage at the hotel; he would see. He left the room and after a little returned with the first volume of the *Arcana Cœlestia,* which contained, as I found on examination, Swedenborg's exposition of the verses of which we had been speaking. I first read the title, which ran as follows:

Arcana Cœlestia—The Heavenly Arcana contained in the Holy Scriptures or Word of the Lord unfolded, beginning with the book of Genesis, together with wonderful things seen in the World of Spirits and in the Heaven of Angels. Translated from the Latin of Emanuel Swedenborg.

I then looked for a preface, the part of a book which usually first engages my attention, but found none. On the first page of the text, however, I found what was a partial substitute for one. It read as follows:

THE BOOK OF GENESIS.

1. That the Word of the Old Testament includes arcana of heaven, and that all its contents, to every particular, regard the Lord, His heaven, the Church, Faith, and the things relating to faith, no man can conceive who only views it from the letter. For the letter, or literal sense, suggests only such things as respect the externals of the Jewish Church, whereas, it everywhere contains internal things which do not in the least appear in those externals, except in a very

few cases, where the Lord revealed and unfolded them to the Apostles—as that sacrifices are significative of the Lord, and that the Land of Canaan and Jerusalem are significative of heaven, on which account they are called the Heavenly Canaan and Jerusalem—and that Paradise has a like signification.

2. But that all and every part of its contents, even to the most minute, not excepting the smallest jot and tittle, signify and involve spiritual and celestial things, is a truth to this day deeply hidden from the Christian world; in consequence of which, little attention is paid to the Old Testament. This truth, however, might appear plainly from this single circumstance; that the Word, being of the Lord, could not possibly be given without containing interiorly such things as relate to Heaven, to the Church, and to Faith. For if this be denied, how can it be called the Word of the Lord or be said to have any life in it? For whence is its life? that is except from hence, that all things in it, both generally and particularly, have relation to the Lord, who is the very life itself? Wherefore, whatsoever does not interiorly regard Him does not live; nay, whatsoever expression in the Word does not involve Him, or in its measure relate to Him, is not divine.

3. Without such a living principle, the Word, as to the letter, is dead. For it is with the Word as with man, who, as all Christians are taught to believe, consists of two parts, an external and an internal. The external man, separate from the internal, is the body, which in such a state of separation is dead; but the internal man is the Lord, and the Word as to the letter alone is like a body without a soul.

4. It is impossible, whilst the mind abides in a literal sense only, to see that it is full of such spiritual contents. Thus in these first chapters of Genesis, nothing is discoverable from the literal sense, but

29

that they treat of the creation of the world and of the Garden of Eden, which is called Paradise, and also of Adam as the first-created man; and scarcely a single person supposes them to relate to anything besides. But that they contain arcana, which were never heretofore revealed, will sufficiently appear from the following pages, where it will be seen that the first chapter of Genesis, in its internal sense, treats of the re-creation of man, or of his regeneration in general and specifically of the Most Ancient Church; and this in such a manner that there is not a syllable which does not represent, signify and involve something spiritual.

5. That this is really the case in regard to the Word, it is impossible for any mortal to know, however, except from the Lord. Wherefore, it is expedient here to premise, that, of the Lord's divine mercy, it has been granted me, now for several years, to be constantly and uninterruptedly in company with spirits and angels, hearing them converse with each other and conversing with them. Hence, it had been permitted me to hear and see things in another life which are astonishing and which have never before come to the knowledge of any man nor entered into his imagination. I have there been instructed concerning different kinds of spirits and the state of souls after death; concerning hell, or the lamentable state of the unfaithful; concerning heaven, or the most happy state of the faithful; and, particularly, concerning the doctrine of faith, which is acknowledged throughout all heaven, on which subjects, by the divine mercy of the Lord, more will be said in the following pages.

Having perused these introductory paragraphs, I turned to chapter 12 to see what the privileged Swede had to say in behalf of Abram. After reciting the chapter at length, he proceeded to give what was entitled "The Internal Sense," and in terms which were calculated to arrest my attention. They ran as follows:

1403. From the first chapter of Genesis, as far as here, or rather to the account of Heber, the narratives are not matters of true history, but compositions in the form of history, signifying, in the internal sense, things celestial and spiritual. In this and the following chapters the narratives are not compositions in the form of history merely, but matters of true history. These, in the internal sense, equally signify things celestial and spiritual; as may appear from this consideration alone, that it is the Word of the Lord.

1404. In these narratives, which are matters of true history, all the declarations and words, and each of them singly, have, in the internal sense, an entirely different signification from that which they bear in the literal sense; and the historical facts themselves are representative. Abram, who is first treated of, represents in general the Lord and in particular the celestial man; Isaac, who is afterwards treated of, in like manner represents in general the Lord and in particular the spiritual man. Jacob, also, in general represents the Lord, and in particular the natural man. Thus they represent the things appertaining to the Lord, to His Kingdom and to His Church.

1405. But the internal sense is of such a nature as has thus far been clearly shown, that in it all things are to be understood, even to the minutest particulars, abstractly from the letter, and just as if the letter did not exist; for in the internal sense is the soul and life of the Word, which does not appear, unless the literal sense is as it were evanescent. It is thus that the angels, by gift from the Lord, have a perception of the Word when it is read by man.

Then follows an exposition of what Swedenborg terms the interior or spiritual meaning of each verse, I might say of almost every word of each verse of the chapter, and occupying forty-five broad octavo pages. I could not make much out of his exegesis; but I was a little disappointed in one respect. Nothing was farther from my thoughts than to suppose that in this book, written over a hundred years ago, of which I had never before seen a copy, and to which, in all my not inconsiderable and varied reading of the English classics, I had rarely seen an allusion, I should find anything that could change or in the least modify my opinion of Abram or of the Bible. I read from curiosity merely, expecting to drop the book as soon as I came to something—and I did not in the least doubt I soon should— that would be so absurd, or improbable, or illogical, as would justify me, without rudeness, in returning the book to my Danish friend with thanks.

Though I understood but imperfectly what I read, I did not find what I was looking for; I found nothing that I could point to with confidence and say, "There, you see your man Swedenborg must have been either a fool or an impostor, if not both." On the other hand, I did find several curious and striking things which piqued my curiosity. For example, his opening comments on the first verse of the chapter showed me that at least I was following a thoughtful guide. I had neither heard nor read anything like it before.

1408. These, and the subsequent circumstances, historically occurred as they are related; but still the historical facts are representative, and each word is significative. The case is the same in all the histor-

ical narratives of the Word, not only those in the books of Moses, but also those in the books of Joshua, of Judges, of Samuel, and of the Kings. In all these, nothing is apparent but a mere history; but although history is related in the literal sense, still in the internal sense are heavenly arcana, which lie concealed within, and which can never be seen so long as the mind, together with the eye, is confined to the historical relations, nor are they revealed until the mind is removed from the literal sense. The Word of the Lord is like a body investing a living soul. The things belonging to the soul do not impress whilst the mind fixes its attention only on corporeal objects, insomuch that the existence of the soul is scarcely credited and still less its immortality; but no sooner is the attention of the mind withdrawn from things corporeal than those belonging to the soul and its life begin to appear. This is the reason, not only that corporeal things must die before man can be born again, or be regenerated, but also that the body itself must die before man can be admitted into heaven and see the things of heaven. So it is with the Word of the Lord; its corporeal parts are the containers of the literal sense, whilst the attention of the mind is fixed on which, the internal contents do not appear; but when the former become as it were dead, then first the latter are presented to view. Nevertheless, the things appertaining to the literal sense are like the things in the body of man, viz.: like the scientifics appertaining to the memory, which are derived from the things of sense, and which form common vessels containing things interior or internal. It may, hence, be known that the vessels are one thing and the essentials contained in the vessels another. The vessels are natural things: the essentials contained in the vessels are things spiritual and celestial. Thus, also, the historical facts related in

33

the Word, and all the particular expressions used in the Word, are common, natural, yea, material vessels, containing in them things spiritual and celestial, and these cannot possibly be brought to view, except by the internal sense. This may appear to every one, solely from this consideration, that many things in the Word are spoken according to appearances, yea, according to the fallacies of the senses; as what is said that the Lord is angry, that He punisheth, that He curseth, that He killeth, and many other things of a like nature; when, nevertheless, the internal sense teaches quite the contrary, namely, that the Lord cannot possibly be angry and punish, much less can He curse and kill. Still, however, to those who, from simplicity of the heart, believe the Word just as they comprehend it in the letter, this is not hurtful, provided they live in charity. The reason is because the Word teaches nothing else than that every one is to live in charity with his neighbor, and to love the Lord above all things, and *they who do this, have the internal contents of the Word within themselves, and then the fallacies arising from the literal sense are easily dispelled.*

This idea, that the Word had degrees of significance which varied and expanded in exact proportion to the spirituality of a man's life, was one that had never crossed my mind before, in a way to distinguish the Bible as a literature from Dante or Plato, and it seemed to me as though there might perhaps be something in it; but what? And how did he know, and where were the proofs? Still I could not say, "this is nonsense; this is unscriptural," though the distinction made between the chapters preceding the twelfth and those following, by which it was claimed that the narratives of the first

34

eleven chapters of the Old Testament, embracing the careers of Adam and Eve, of Cain and Abel, the deluge, the building of the tower of Babel, etc., "were not matters of true history," had a somewhat heretical not to say profane ring. I was, however, so pleased to find that any one had found a way of retaining his faith in the divine origin of the Bible, without being obliged to accept its account of the creation as history, that I did not feel like having Swedenborg burned as a heretic for that. In spite of these redeeming features in his writings, however, I did not in the least despair of bringing him to the stake before I had done with him. I persuaded myself that he had built up a theosophy from his imagination, and I knew enough to know that no human imagination was capable of producing anything of that kind that would not bristle with weak points, which could not all escape the penetration of even so poor a theologian as I was. So I turned to other places to see what he said, for example, of Abram's subsequent misrepresentation to Abimelech, what of Isaac's repetition of the same fraud in Gerar; of the tower of Babel; of Hagar; of Jacob and his mother's scheme to defraud Esau of his birthright; what of Jacob's method of enriching himself at the expense of his father-in-law, Laban; of Rachel's fib to her father about the images, and so on. In this way I spent the entire day, I looked through the whole volume. Much of it was too mystical to be intelligible to me then; but, to my mortification, it began to dawn upon me that it was unintelligible to me, much for the same reason as the *Mechanique Céleste* would have been. While I ran upon many things that were quite new to me and seemed wise, I did not find

35

anything upon which I could move to put the author out of Court. On the contrary, the desire to read on, grew by what it fed on, and begat a longing to know something of the author's personality.

When Mr. Kjerulff came in to dinner that evening, I said to him that I had spent the day with his friend Swedenborg, but that the value of what I had read depended so largely upon the tenor of his life and the character he had borne in the flesh that I felt as though, before spending any more time upon his works, I would like to be enlightened on these points. Mr. Kjerulff, thereupon, ran over the prominent events of Swedenborg's life in a rather enthusiastic strain, as it seemed to me, and wound up by assuring me, in substance, that he doubted if in the history of our race another man could be found, who had ever succeeded in delivering himself more completely from the sway of the World, the Flesh and the Devil. I asked if he had any biography of Swedenborg. He replied, after a little reflection, that he believed he had in his luggage a collection of documents relating to Swedenborg compiled by a Mr. Bush, of New York, where he said I would find, in the testimony of Swedenborg's contemporaries, the best of evidence in regard to his singular purity of life, his conspicuous elevation of character, and the completeness of his consecration to the service of the Master. I asked if the Bush to whom he referred was the professor of Oriental languages in the New York University and a Presbyterian clergyman, who had written commentaries on the Bible. All he knew about his antecedents was that he had been a clergyman, though of what denomination he did not recollect, and that since becoming ac-

36

quainted with the writings of Swedenborg he had withdrawn from it, whichever it was, and was then settled as pastor of the New Church (Swedenborgian) in Brooklyn. As I had long known Prof. Bush, and esteemed him very highly for his eminence, both as a scholar and as a Christian, I was greatly surprised to learn that he had been dabbling in heresy. Of one thing, however, I was quite sure, that he was entirely incapable of lending himself to any sort of imposture, and that absolute confidence might be placed in the good faith of anything published with his name or with his sanction. The fact that he had so far separated himself from the Church organization in which he had been bred, in which he had worked with distinction as pastor and author for many of the best years of his life, and had sacrificed to his convictions what to him no doubt seemed and was, in a worldly point of view, his all, increased my interest in his book and its hero. So I begged Mr. Kjerulff to let me see it. He promptly complied with my wishes. The book was entitled, "Documents Concerning Swedenborg," and consisted chiefly of letters and publications of Swedenborg's contemporaries, showing the estimate and reasons for the estimate in which he was held by them. I read the book almost at a sitting. My first feeling when I laid it down was of mingled surprise and mortification that I had lived till then in such dense ignorance of the career and work of so remarkable a man, at once so great and so good as Swedenborg was there shown to have been, while I had spent so much of my life in trying to make myself familiar with the lives of men, who were unworthy to unloose the

37

latchets of his shoes. Whatever doubts I had entertained of Swedenborg's good faith and sincerity, this book effectually dispelled. He might have been subject to illusions, but I had no longer any suspicions of his being an impostor. These convictions naturally increased my curiosity to know more of his writings, and especially of his theology, though my curiosity was still of a purely intellectual origin and character.

IV

THOUGH getting to be somewhat absorbed by this new acquaintance, I did not forget that I was a long way from home; that the time I had proposed to be absent had already expired; that I had not heard either from my family or from my business colleagues since I left New York, nor had I any reason to presume they had heard from me. Mr. Kjerulff and I had studied up the destination and plans of every vessel in the harbor of St. Thomas to no profit, till at last we opened negotiations with a skipper in command of a fore and aft schooner of 130 tons or thereabouts, owned in Baltimore, to take us to some port in the United States. As he could get no freight, for which he had been hoping, from or to any Spanish port, on account of the cholera, he finally decided, if we would take passage with him, to go to New Orleans and look for a freight there. An arrangement with him was concluded; we laid in a stock of extra provisions, and, with more alacrity than I ever left any port before or since save one, we took leave of St. Thomas bound for New Orleans. Before sailing, however, I begged Mr. Kjerulff to take with him all the books he had by or about Swedenborg. With this request he very obligingly complied.

Our voyage was prolonged both by calms and storms, and more than twenty days elapsed between the time of our departure from St. Thomas and my arrival at New York. I do not recollect but one day in all that interval —a day that I spent in New Orleans, where the editor of the *Picayune* drove me out to Lake Ponchartrain— that I did not pore from ten to twelve hours over these writings. In fact, they absorbed all my time that was not devoted to eating and sleeping. It would not be possible to convey to any one, who had not had a similar experience, the effect they produced upon me, the almost insane appetite with which I devoured them, the complete revolution that they wrought in all my opinions about spiritual matters, and especially about the Bible. Though, like the blind man in the gospel, I as yet only saw men as trees walking, before I reached home I had acquired a thorough conviction that "these were not the words of him who hath a devil," and that Swedenborg was "a scribe instructed unto the Kingdom of Heaven." It seemed to me that every line I read removed some difficulty, cleared up some doubt, illuminated some mystery, revealed spiritual wealth in the Word of which before I had no conception. If I had become possessed of Aladdin's lamp or had discovered a new continent, I could not have been more completely rapt, more wildly intoxicated with my acquisition. I felt literally that whereas I was blind now I saw; as if my eyes had opened to a world of which till then I had only seen the reflection or shadow. Saul of Tarsus could not have been more utterly surprised and carried away

39

when "there fell from his eyes as it had been scales and he received sight forthwith," than I was as my mind was opened to the new truths which were revealed to me during this voyage. Before reaching New Orleans I found myself on my knees, exclaiming, "Lord, I believe, help Thou my unbelief." The terms in which the Rev. John Clowes described the impression produced on him by his first perusal of Swedenborg's "True Christian Religion," would at one time have seemed to me rhapsodical and extravagant. They now seem to me perfectly natural and not in the least exaggerated.*

* The Reverend John Clowes, formerly fellow of Trinity College, Cambridge, England, was the Rector of St. John's church, Manchester, for sixty-two years. He was born at Manchester in October, 1743, and died the 28th of May, 1831. He says: "It is impossible for any language to express the full effect wrought in my mind by the perusal of this wonderful book. Suffice it, therefore, to observe that in proceeding from the chapter on the Creator and Creation to the succeeding chapters on the Redeemer and Redemption, on the Divine Trinity, on the Sacred Scriptures or Word of God, on the Decalogue, on Faith, on Charity, on Free-will, on Repentance, on Reformation and Regeneration, on Imputation, on Baptism, on the Holy Supper, on the Consummation of the Age, the Advent of the Lord, and the New Heaven and the New Church, it seemed as if a continually increasing blaze of new and recreating light was poured forth on the delighted understanding, opening it to the contemplation of the most sublime mysteries of wisdom, and convincing it of the being of a God, of the existence of an internal world, of the interior sanctities of the Holy Scriptures, of the true nature of creation, redemption and regeneration, in a manner and degree, and with a force of satisfactory evidence, in which those interesting subjects had never been viewed before. The mind, therefore, was no longer perplexed about the proper Object of its worship, because it was enlightened to see clearly, as by the light of a meridian sun, that Jesus Christ, in His Divine Humanity, is that Object, He being the Creator from eternity, thus containing in His own Divine Person the Sacred Trinity of Father, Son and Holy Spirit; the Father being His hidden essence, the Son His manifested existence, and the Holy Spirit His proceeding operation. In like manner all difficulties and doubts were removed respecting the Sacred Scriptures, or Word of God,

When I left the steamer at Cincinnati to take the train East it became necessary for me to part with my good friend Kjerulff* and his books. As I was to be detained a few hours in Cincinnati, I lost no time in looking up a bookstore, where I was fortunate enough to find a nice copy of Swedenborg's *Divine Love and Wisdom* and of *Divine Providence* bound together. The price I paid for it led me to suspect that it was not regarded by the proprietor as very valuable merchandise, but I would not have exchanged it for any other book in his shop. In fact, I felt then as though I should never care to read any other books but Swedenborg's and the Bible. I devoted the daylight hours during the remainder of my journey to my new treasure, every line of which seemed to set a new star in the heavens for me. By the time I reached home, though not quite clear in my mind about the nature or extent of Swedenborg's illumination, if specially illuminated at all, nor indeed caring much to know, not doubting that he believed he was, I had got over not only all my difficulties about Christ's mysterious birth and miracles, but I had become equally well satisfied of the Divine

through the bright and heretofore unseen manifestation of their spiritual and interior contents, by virtue of which discovery apparent inconsistencies vanished, apparent contradictions were reconciled, and what before seemed trivial and nugatory, assumed a new and interesting aspect; while the whole volume of Revelation was seen to be full of sanctity, of wisdom and of love from its Divine Author, and also to be in perpetual connection with that Author, who is its inmost soul—its essential Spirit and Life."

* Mr. Kjerulff died in 1874 in the island of Santa Cruz, where he had resumed the practice of his profession. Two daughters survive him. A letter written by his daughter Rose, giving an account of her father's death, will be found on page 117.

authority of the twelve chapters of Genesis over which I had so often stumbled. If there were any parts of the Bible about the Divine origin of which I was less clear, I presumed they were given for our edification, but upon what precise authority I did not pretend to know, nor then much care. I felt like one who had sold all he had and bought a pearl of great price, but at such a bargain that he did not care to wait for his change.

I embraced an early opportunity, upon my return, to look up Dr. Bush. I found him where I had occasionally seen him before, in what he called his "den," a small room in the upper part of the Morse Building, since replaced by a more imposing structure bearing the same name. The room was nearly full of books. He had reserved a place for himself at his desk and scant room besides to seat a visitor or two. I was much interested, of course, in hearing from his own lips of the revolution through which he had passed. He seemed very happy and well assured that he had found "the Way, the Truth and the Life." It turned out that he had already for several years had the advantage of Swedenborg's teachings. In a little pamphlet which he published about 1845, entitled, "Statement of Reasons for Embracing the Doctrines and Disclosures of Swedenborg," he had given an interesting account of the circumstances which first turned his studies specially in that direction. As the "Statement" is now pretty much forgotten, and as the journey his mind travelled, the difficulties he encountered and the processes by which he surmounted them were in many respects similar to my own, and I suspect of most persons who have found in Swedenborg, as he had done, deliverance from spiritual disorders for which the Church, in which we had been reared, had neither cure nor anodyne, I cannot doubt that those who have followed me thus far will be edified by it.

"In the retrospect of the last five or six years of my moral and intellectual life, I am compelled to fix upon the date when I was first led to question the received doctrine of the Resurrection, as the point from which my progress really began to tend towards the New Church, although then profoundly ignorant of the fact. I had previously acquired no precise knowledge of Swedenborg's system, nor formed any intelligent estimate of his character. With the mass of the Christian world, I had contented myself with the vague impression of his having been a man of respectable talents and attainments, but who had unhappily fallen into a kind of monomania, which made him the victim of strange delusions and dreams—the honest but real dupe of the wildest phantasies in respect to the state of man after death, and the constituent nature of Heaven and Hell. As to anything like a consistent or rational philosophy of man's nature or the constitution of the universe, I should as soon have looked for it in the Koran of Mahomet or the Vedas of the Hindoos, or what I then deemed the senseless ravings of Jacob Behmen. Having never read his works but in fragmentary extracts, I was unprepared to recognize in him anything beyond the character of a well-meaning mystic, who had given forth to the world a strange medley of hallucinations that could never be supposed to meet with acceptance, except in minds which had received some touch of a similar mania, and which had lost, if they ever possessed, the power of accurately discriminating between visions and verities. Such was my general estimate of the man up to the time when I had become

43

settled in the belief that the current dogma of the *resurrection of the material body* was a gratuitous hypothesis, equally unsupported by a sound interpretation of Scripture, or by the fair inductions of reason. The grounds of this opinion I have given to the public in a work ("Anastasis, etc.") expressly devoted to the subject.

"I had already begun to announce my conclusions on this head in a course of public lectures delivered in this city and elsewhere, maintaining that the true resurrection took place at death, when, at the close of one of these lectures in an eastern city, a lady incidentally remarked to me that the views I had advanced bore a striking analogy with those of Swedenborg on the same theme, and intimated her impression that I must have been conversant with his works. The supposition was unfounded, but my curiosity was excited, and I determined, at the first favorable opportunity, to acquaint myself with the system, and thus supply a conscious desideratum in my knowledge.

"Not many months elapsed before a copy of Noble's Appeal in behalf of the views of the New Church fell into my hands, by the perusal of which I was very deeply impressed. I was compelled to form an entirely new estimate of the man and of the system. I not only saw my own general views of the nature of the resurrection abundantly confirmed, and illustrated, and planted upon the basis of a philosophy and psychology which I still deem impregnable, but an exhibition also of the doctrine of the Lord's Second Advent, which came home to my convictions with a peculiar power of demonstration. I was struck, too, in the perusal of this work, with the *Scriptural* character of the evidence adduced in support of the doctrines. I had previously no adequate conception of the amount of testimony from this source going to sustain the lead-

44

ing positions of the New Church scheme, and to this hour I do not scruple to regard Noble's Appeal as an unanswerable defence of the system.

"Hitherto, however, I had read nothing of Swedenborg's own writings, excepting occasional detached paragraphs. The '*Heaven and Hell*' shortly afterwards fell under my perusal. I read it with profound interest, but still with great abatements from a full conviction of its truth. I was rather disposed, on the whole, to admit the possibility of the psychological state into which Swedenborg declared himself to be brought, and which alone could make him cognizant of the realities of the spiritual world, because I saw that a similar immission into that world had been granted to the prophets and apostles, which showed that such a state could exist, and if it had once existed, I saw not why it might not again, provided sufficient reasons could be pleaded for it; and the reasons alleged I felt to be sufficient *if* they were but sound; a question that I felt myself willing seriously to consider, but which I think the mass of the Christian world is not. I found, however, in my perusal of the work, such a violence done to all my preconceptions of that world, that I doubted exceedingly the absolute reliableness of his statements. I could not help distrusting the lucidity of his perceptions. I was continually haunted by the suspicion that his preformed ideas on the subject had both shaped and colored his visions. This was more especially the case in regard to his descriptions of celestial and infernal scenery. I had the greatest difficulty imaginable in conceiving the possibility that any objects similar to those with which we are conversant here should even *appear* to exist there. Again and again did I propose to myself the question, What kind of an entity is a spiritual house, animal or bird—a spiritual mountain, garden, grove, or tree—a spiritual

45

cavern, lake, or stream—not dreaming that these things exist there by the very laws of the human mind, as outbirths or emanations of the interior spirit, and as living representatives of its affections and thoughts? It did not then occur to me that a spirit dislodged from the body must, from the necessity of the case, be introduced into the midst of *spiritual* realities, and that these cannot in the nature of things be any other than what Swedenborg describes them to be—that is, they must be what we should term *mental creations* or *projections.* A little deeper reflection would have then taught me, as it has since done, to assent freely to the truth of Swedenborg's statement, that thoughts are actual though not material *substances,* and that to spirits, that alone can be *substantial* which is *spiritual,* and consequently that alone can be *real.* We, indeed, in common parlance, reverse these terms, and denominate that *substantial* which is *material,* and which comes under the cognizance of the external senses. But the spirit, on leaving the body, leaves the region of dead matter, and comes into a sphere where itself and its emanations are the *real substances* or the *substantial realities.* Consequently, what is here *subjective* becomes there *objective.*

*   *   *   *   *   *   *   *

"This I am aware, will find with many but a slow admission, on its first announcement, from their having been always accustomed to regard these manifestations of mind as simple *acts, exercises, operations,* etc. But let the matter be pondered, and judgment rendered, whether the fact be not actually so. How can anything exist which is not a *substance?* How can anything that exists *act,* but by the putting forth of its qualities and functions *as a substance?* The sun *acts* by the emission of its light and heat. Are

46

not the light and heat of the sun a part of its *substance?* A flower *acts* by sending forth a sphere of fragrance. Is not the fragrance as real a *substance* as the flower, though vastly more rarefied and ethereal? So of the human spirit. A man's thoughts and mental images are the goings forth of the *substance* of his being; they are as substantial *as* his being; and if a spirit himself can be an objective reality to another spirit, his intellectual conceptions, for the same reason, must be equally objective. Consequently, nothing more is needed, for one's being introduced in the most splendid celestial scenery, than to find himself surrounded by the mental creations prompted by the pure and angelic affections of the countless multitudes which constitute that kingdom. These *must* be beautiful, because they originate in a moral state of the inner man, which can only be represented by objects of a corresponding character; and that they are *real,* arises from the nature and necessity of the case. Spiritual objects must be the *real* objects to a spirit. The infernal scenery, though a counterpart to this, depends upon the same law.

"A great advance was accordingly made towards a full reception of the disclosure of Swedenborg, when the objections on this score were overcome. I saw that here was a rational and philosophical theory of the dominant conditions of the other life; and yet it was evidently a revelation of such a nature as to transcend the utmost grasp of the unassisted human faculties. The inference, therefore, was not only fair but irresistible, that Swedenborg was brought into a preternatural state, in order to his being enabled to make it; and the admission of this was a virtual admission of the main item of his claim—the claim of having been divinely empowered to lay open the verities of man's future existence, and the essential nature of Heaven and Hell.

47

"This primary fact, then, having been established to my own satisfaction, I was, of course, very strongly disposed to listen with the deepest respect to whatever other reports he brought from that world of mystery and of marvel; although I was still very far—as indeed I hope ever to be—from a blind surrender of my own judgment, as to every point of his announcements. I was not yet prepared to receive the distinctive features of his theology, and more especially was I stumbled by his unsparing critiques upon the doctrine of Justification by Faith alone, which I had been taught to regard as the grand tenet established by the Reformation, and which I supposed to be true, of course, simply from its having been the result of that struggle, which is so often spoken of as the *glorious* Reformation from the errors of Popery. I had yet to learn that there were a great many things in the Reformation that need much further *reforming*. So also in regard to the peculiar views advanced respecting the true nature of the Atonement, from which the current doctrine of Justification is inseparable. It was long before I could so entirely emancipate my mind from traditional sentiments, as to embrace fully what I now regard as the far more Scriptural views of the New Church on that subject, to wit, that the atonement was what is signified by the word—*reconciliation*—God reconciling the world to Himself, instead of reconciling Himself to the world.

"But the great rock of offence with me was the interior or spiritual sense of the Word. This, I was strongly assured, even if there were to some extent a basis of truth on which it rested, was yet carried to an entirely fanciful extreme in Swedenborg's interpretations; and I had scarcely a doubt that if I ever accepted the system as a whole, it would still be with a reservation on this score. One who is at all acquainted with the general scheme, will see at once from this, that I had thus far failed to apprehend the true genius of the Science of Correspondences, on which it rests, and from which it flows by inevitable sequence. The truth of this science, however, gradually loomed up more and more to view, as I became more clearly aware of the spiritual nature of man, and of the fundamental fact, that all natural things are pervaded, acted, moulded, vivified by the influx of spiritual causes."

With **Dr.** Bush I afterward had many pleasant and edifying talks. I promptly procured a copy of the "Arcana Cœlestia," and, as I felt the need of them, the other theological writings of Swedenborg. I also looked up the Church frequented chiefly by students of Swedenborg in Thirty-fifth street, in which the Rev. Chauncey Giles was then preaching, and which I have habitually attended since when in town.

V

HIGHLY as I valued Swedenborg as a Commentator and an opener of the Word, I was not as yet prepared to accept him as a revelator. Accustomed to regard the Bible as a unit and unique, as a great light with which God had endowed His people, I hesitated to believe that His revelations could be incomplete, or could ever require supplementation. It seemed more probable that Swedenborg had read the Word more carefully, had penetrated its mysteries more profoundly, and developed truths equally accessible to any person endowed with

49

18806

equal genius and equally free from sectarian delusions and moral infirmities. If the Word required the light which Swedenborg professed to shed upon it, why was it withheld so long, and why had not preceding generations been permitted to profit by it?

This question reminds one of an Italian who wrote a book to prove that the four new planets discovered by Galileo were imaginary, and concluded by asking: "Of what use are they? Astrologers have got on very well without these new planets hitherto. There can be no reason, therefore, for their starting into existence now."

I ultimately found my answer where any earnest seeker for truth, for truth's sake, may find a deliverance from all doubts which obstruct his spiritual evolution— in the Bible itself. The objection to a new revelation in the eighteenth century I found, could, with equal propriety, be made to the revelations made by our Saviour and by John, nay by Abraham, by Moses and by all the prophets. Over a thousand years intervened between the inditing of the Ten Commandments on the one hand, and the prophecies of Malachi on the other, during which interval the Lord appears to have been in frequent, not to say constant, commmunication with His people. The call of Abraham occurred B. C. 1921. The prophecies of Malachi were written B. C. 420. During this interval of more than fifteen centuries the Bible records over fifty distinct revelations of the Divine Will to as many different persons and on as many different occasions. I have taken the trouble to prepare a list of some of the recipients of these revelations, with a reference to the text where they are recorded.

50

			CHAP.	VERSE.
29.	To Jahaziel	See 2 Chron.,	20	14
30.	" Zechariah	" "	24	20
31.	" Haggai	" Ezra,	5	1
32.	" Ezra	" "	6	14
	" "	" "	7	6
33.	" The man of God that came to Amaziah ...	" "	25	7
34.	" Prophet sent to Amaziah	" 2 Chron.,	25	15
35.	" Jeremiah	" Jeremiah,	1	1
36.	" Nehemiah	" Nehemiah,	1	1
37.	" Esther	" Esther.		
38.	" Job	" Job,	38	1
39.	" Ezekiel	" Ezekiel,	1	1
40.	" Daniel	" Daniel.		
41.	" Hosea	" Hosea,	1	1
42.	" Joel	" Joel	1	1
43.	" Amos	" Amos,	1	3
44.	" Obadiah	" Obadiah	1	1
45.	" Jonah	" Jonah,	1	1
46.	" Micah	" Micah,	1	1
47.	" Nahum	" Nahum.		
48.	" Habakkuk	" Habak.,	1	1
49.	" Zephaniah	" Zeph.,	1	1
50.	" Malachi	" Malachi,	1	1
	" Haggai	" Haggai,	1	1
51.	" Iddo	" "	2	1

To these may be added the Psalms, in which Jesus is often the speaker. These poems, too, are the work of several inspired authors, and appeared not at one time, but at intervals covering a period of not less than a thousand years.

The New Testament equally presents a succession of

revelations, made to as many different persons and at
different times. Here is a list of some of them:

			CHAP.	VERSE.
1. To Joseph	See Matthew,	1	20
2. " John the Baptist	" "	3	15
" "	" "	2	14
3. " Simon Peter	" "		
4. " Andrew	" "		
5. " James	" "		
6. " John the son of Zeb- edee	" "		
7. " Philip	" "	10	2
8. " Bartholomew	" "		
9. " Thomas	" "		
10. " James	" "		
11. " Thaddeus	" "		
12. " Simon the Canaanite...	" "		
13. " Judas Iscariöt	" "		
14. " Paul	" Acts,	9	6
15. " Philip	" "	8	26
16. " Mark	" Mark.		
17. " Luke	" Luke.		
18. " Stephen	" Acts,	7	55
19. " John the Divine	" Revelation.		

Here we have in the Old and New Testaments together no less than seventy different revelations made
by the Lord to almost as many different persons and
on almost as many different occasions, within a period
of sixteen hundred years. What reason was there for
supposing that John, any more than Malachi, or than
Isaiah, or than Solomon, or than David, or than Joshua,
or than Abraham, or than Moses, was to be the last to
whom He would reveal Himself? And would it not

have seemed, reasoning from the past, more surprising, had He not made any farther revelation of Himself in the next seventeen centuries than that He did? What did He mean when He said to His disciples, "I have many things to say unto you, but ye cannot bear them now," if not that when His disciples were fit to know more of righteousness, temperance and judgment to come, more would be revealed to them—that they would hear from Him again?

As for the agent through whom to make new revelations, I had no difficulty in acknowledging the entire sufficiency and fitness of Swedenborg, nor does my memory suggest the name of any one man who lived before or since the time of Jesus more thoroughly equipped for such an extraordinary commission; of any medium through which the light of Divine truth would pass with less refraction. It is not possible to find any authority for supposing that any of those who had been previously selected by the Lord as such media possessed any qualifications for their mission which, *mutatis mutandis,* Swedenborg did not possess for his, while, humanly speaking, it is doing none of the others any injustice to say that for his peculiar mission he possessed many qualifications which all the others presumably lacked. At his maturity, he was the most illustrious scientific man living. He consecrated his extraordinary talents to the loftiest and most elevating uses. He was a favorite of his king because of his usefulness; there were hardly any worldly honors or political distinctions he did not receive, to which he might not have aspired. He laid them all down to devote himself exclusively to the work to which he believed the Lord had called him,

54

neither receiving nor desiring any reward from the world for his labors or his sacrifices. He not only printed all his books at his private expense, but as fast as printed gave them all away, mostly to libraries, to await the time when the world should realize its need of them, having implicit faith that the Lord would in His own good time breathe into them the breath of life.*

I had no longer any difficulty therefore with what at first seemed like an impeachment of the completeness and sufficiency of the Bible, and I came to regard every revelation of spiritual truth, from Moses down the ages, as merely successive liftings of veils, the dispersing of clouds, for the revelation of vital truths of which all nature is the Divine Scripture, and the Bible its translation and interpreter, but which the children of men are prepared to accept only, as it were, by instalments. Neither had I any farther difficulty in regarding Swedenborg as a suitable agent for the reception of a new revelation, as much so as any of the twelve Apostles appear to have been.

* Concerning Volume I, John Lewis states in Document 258, p. 494, "This gentleman (*i. e.* Swedenborg) with indefatigable pains and labour spent one whole year in studying and writing the first volume of *the Arcana Cœlestia;* was at the expense of two hundred pounds to print it, and also advanced two hundred pounds more for the printing of the second volume; and when he had done this, he gave express orders, that all the money that should arise in the sale of this large work should be given toward the charge of the propagation of the gospel." He was as indifferent about the fame, as about the pecuniary returns his book would yield. The first public notice of the *Arcana Cœlestia* and of five other treatises published in 1758, appeared in Sweden in 1763, thirteen years after the appearance of the first volume of the *Arcana.*

55

VI

In the perusal of these pages it will doubtless occur to the reader to ask what, after all, did I learn from Swedenborg of substantial value, that I did not know or might not have learned from the pulpits of the Churches open to me in New York? Especially what, if anything, to which I can attribute the great change wrought in my views of my relations to the Godhead within those few short weeks? It would require volumes to answer this question fully; but I can state in a brief space some of the most striking and comprehensive truths for which, by God's mercy, I think I am indebted to these writings.

First. They apprised me of the fact that I, in common with most professing Christians, had been all my life a pagan, believing or acting as though I believed in a plurality of Gods. While at school in Troy and afterwards at Trinity College, Hartford—it was called Washington College in my time—I had been required to attend the Episcopal Church, and every Sunday to repeat what is termed in the Prayer Book, The Apostles' Creed, in which I proclaimed my belief in—

(1) God the Father Almighty, Maker of heaven and earth.

(2) In Jesus Christ, His only Son our Lord, who was conceived by the Holy Ghost, born of the Virgin Mary, etc.

(3) In the Holy Ghost.

(4) In the Holy Catholic Church.

(5) In the Communion of Saints.

(6) In the forgiveness of sins.

(7) In the resurrection of the body.

(8) In the life everlasting.

Here were eight separate articles of belief, including a belief in at least three separate and distinct Gods, whom I was educated to recognize, and to whom I was to address my prayers. Jesus Christ, the Son, was just as distinct from the Father in this profession of faith as the Communion of Saints was distinct from the forgiveness of sins, or from the resurrection of the body. The Holy Ghost was apparently a third person, equally distinct from both the Father and Son. When I attempted to pray I was always perplexed to know which of the three I was appealing to or ought to address. This difficulty got me some years later into the habit for a time, of attending the Unitarian Church. As I advanced in life, and in blindness perhaps, I used to address my petitions to God the Father, closing my eyes, as it were, to the other two, to avoid confusion.

If I am not greatly mistaken, the impression generally prevails among what are called orthodox Christians, that there is a sort of graded Godhead, to which the Roman Catholics add the Virgin Mary, and now I believe the Pope; to which the Greek Church adds the Czar; the Moslems, Mahomet, and the Mormons, Joe Smith. I am indebted to Swedenborg for showing me the way out of this polytheistical tangle, and making perfectly intelligible to me the great central truth of Christian faith, that there is but one God, in Whom, as Swedenborg describes it, there is a trinity of person, not of persons; that Jesus was Jehovah Himself re-

57

vealed to us in the measure proportioned to our needs and capacities for receiving Him, just as the light and heat which enter our windows are the sun passed through an atmosphere several miles deep to prevent their blinding or burning us. In this way I comprehended how in Christ was the fullness of the Godhead bodily; how the Father, Son and Holy Ghost are united in the One Divine Person of the Saviour, forming One Divine Being, in like manner as the soul, body and their joint operation in man, form one human being.*

* This view was presented very effectively by the Rev. Mr. Clowes, in the preface to his Commentaries on Luke, more than half a century ago. "When it is said of the Father that He created the world, of the Son that He redeemed it, and of the Holy Ghost that He sanctified it, and when these three, viz., the Father, Son and Holy Ghost, are called distinct persons, and have distinct offices allotted to them, and lay claim to a distinct worship, what is the necessary result of all these distinctions but to establish a monstrous tritheism, fraught with the most mischievous consequences by its direct tendencies to distract the mind of the sincere worshipper, to perplex him as to the proper object of his adoration, since it is absolutely impossible for the human mind to pay its debt of religious gratitude, love, praise and supplication to more than one Divine Being.

"To this denial of the Incarnate God of the sole exclusive Divinity, the division of the Godhead into three persons and in the allotment of a distinct office and operation to each person— to the Father, the act of creation; to the Son, the act of redemption; and to the Holy Ghost, the act of sanctification—may be ascribed an incalculable multitude of misconceptions and theological delusions, among which are conspicuous the mistaken notions of an imputed righteousness, of an arbitrary election on the part of God, of justification by faith alone, of salvation by immediate mercy. In what Church in Christendom are its members taught even to-day—save the New Church—to address their prayers directly to Jesus Christ, who has so expressly said, "Come unto Me; abide in Me; without Me ye can do nothing"? (See, also, John xiv. 6.) In what Church are we taught to believe the Humanity of Jesus Christ to be a Divine Humanity, in and through which the invisible Godhead is made visible, the unknown God is made known, the unapproachable Godhead is rendered approachable, and thus the penitent sin-

58

Second. I first learned from Swedenborg that the Atonement was not, as I had always been taught, a reconciliation of God with the world through a barbarous and unnatural traffic arrangement, but a reconciliation of the world with God; an at-one-ment effected through the intervention of the Lord's Divine Humanity. If the Father and Son really were one person, and the unity of the Godhead assumed that they were, of course neither could feel any resentment towards sinners not equally shared by the other, nor could either have any claims of justice which were not common to both. The Son, therefore, could not but feel as much wrath towards sinners as the Father, and the Father as much compassion for them and solicitude for their salvation as the Son. So that the idea of crucifying either to satisfy the honour of the other, was not only at war with any rational conception of God, the Good, the Great, the Just, but struck a fatal blow at the unity of the Godhead. Such a scheme of redemption requires at least two Gods, or it strips Christ of His Divinity, in which latter case His death ceases to be the infinite

ner always has access to his Heavenly Father? And yet we are assured that "I and the Father are one," John x. 30; "Believe Me, that I am in the Father, and the Father in Me," John xiv. 6-7, 9-11; "I am the door of the sheep—by Me, if any man enter, he shall be saved, and shall go in and out and find his pasture," John x. 7-9.

In what Church is it taught to-day that the Jesus of the New Testament is identical with the Jehovah of the Old? Yet, see Isaiah xxv. 9–40, 3–5–10.—*Preface to the Gospel According to St. Luke, translated from the original Greek, and illustrated by extracts from the theological writings of Emanuel Swedenborg, together with notes and observations by the translator, annexed to each chapter, by the late Rev. J. Clowes, M. A., Rector of St. John's Church, Manchester, and Fellow of Trinity College, Cambridge, who was a member and pastor in full standing of the established Church of England until his death.*

sacrifice which is claimed to have been the stipulated price of our redemption.

Third. In clearing up my ideas on the Atonement, Swedenborg helped me to see that Heaven and Hell are not places, but states or conditions of the soul; that no sinner, whatever he believes, or thinks he believes, can experience the joys of Heaven, except by ceasing to be a sinner; and that this change is wrought, not as I had been taught, from outside of him, or in and through another being by transfer or imputation, but by "a life according to the commandments"; by works as well as faith. He must actually be inhabited by the righteousness which saves and justifies. I had been accustomed to think that, when I was created, I was delivered over to the world like a plough from its factory, or a steamer from the shipyard; that my Creator was to have no more to do with me, at least until the last assize, than the maker of the plough and of the steamer have to do with them; that I had been wound up, as it were, to run like a clock for a few years, more or less, and that I was to be the real author of everything I did or thought until I should have "run down"—or like Job, "I should lie down in the dark." It was Swedenborg that first brought home to me the conviction that every sin and every sinful propensity has its origin in this self-love, in this sense of self-sufficiency, in this primeval ambition to be as Gods; that it was only by expelling, and only so fast as we do expel this selfhood from our hearts, that the Lord could come in and dwell with us. It was not till I began to explore my heart and study the motives of my conduct by the light of this fearful revelation, so new to me, though it lies

60

on the very surface of all Christ's teaching and example, that I began to realize how selfish and worldly my life had been from the beginning; how habitually I had appropriated to myself the credit of anything I thought I had done well; how ingeniously I excused and justified what I had done wrong; with how little charity I had judged those whose conduct wounded what I thought to be my interests, my vanity, or my pride; how little concern I had felt for the happiness and welfare of others compared with that I felt for my own; how impracticable seemed the Divine injunction to do unto others as I would have others do to me; how readily I thought evil of those who differed with me in opinion; how slow to run to the relief of a fellow sinner waylaid and overcome by temptation, and left bleeding by the roadside, to suffer, and perhaps to perish, for lack of timely sympathy and succor. I now realized for the first time that the whole of the work of regeneration consisted in expelling the self-hood which, with the crew of devils in its service, was always trying to persuade me that it was my own breath I drew, my own thought I used, my own work in which I triumphed. It was this self-hood which urged me to conciliate the self-hood of others and which I yearned to have others conciliate in me; it was to this self-hood that I found political agitators and aspirants, philanthropists and reformers, made their most successful appeals. As I watched and became more conversant with this infirmity, I found, to my astonishment, that to its head-quarters might be traced every sinful thought, lust and act which obstructs the Lord in the effort He is always making to re-unite us with Him, and to perfect His image in us; that it was the germ of all dissension, disease, misery and crime in human society, and that the highest, not to say the only ambition which any mortal can afford to indulge, is to pursue and extirpate this self-hood—this *proprium,* as Swedenborg most appropriately terms it—as persistently and unrelentingly and unsparingly as the Israelites were instructed to pursue and exterminate the inhabitants of Canaan, who, Swedenborg tells us, represent the several classes of enemies that beset every human soul.*

* Swedenborg's views of the *proprium* or self-hood, which figure more or less conspicuously in all his writings, may be gathered from a few extracts upon that subject taken from his *Arcana Cœlestia.* "Man's *proprium* is in itself dead, and no one has life from himself, as is shown so clearly in the world of spirits, that evil spirits who love nothing but the *proprium,* and obstinately insist that they live from themselves, are convinced by sensible experience, and forced to confess that they do not live from themselves. It has been especially permitted me now for several years to become acquainted with the human *proprium* and it has been granted to me to perceive clearly that I could think nothing from myself, but that every idea or thought entered by influx, and sometimes, how and where this influx entered. The man, therefore, who supposes that he lives from himself, is in the false, and in consequence appropriates to himself everything evil and false, which he would never do, were he to believe according to the truth of the case." *Arcana Cœlestia,* 150.

A. C. 154. "Nothing evil and false can possibly exist which is not the *proprium,* for the *proprium* of man is evil itself, and hence man is nothing but evil and falsity. This was demonstrated to me by the fact that when the *proprium* of man is presented to view in the world of spirits, it appears so deformed that it is impossible to detect anything more ugly, although with a difference, according to the nature of the *proprium,* so that he to whom the things of his *proprium* are visibly exhibited is struck with horror, and wishes to flee from himself as from a devil."

"It requires but little attention in any one to discover that woman was not made out of the rib of man (Gen. ii. 22.) and that deeper arcana are here implied than any person has heretofore been aware of. It must be plain, also, that by the woman

Fourth. It was Swedenborg who first made me comprehend and realize that all causes are spiritual; and all phenomena were only effects; that all things which exist in the spiritual world are the direct or indirect causes of all those effects, that the internal or spiritual man and the external of natural man are related to each other as cause and effect, the causes of all things operating through the internal man and all effects through the external man, and that whatever takes place from any cause, takes place from and according to some law of the Divine Providence.

Fifth. From Swedenborg I first obtained an idea of Heaven and Hell, that seemed not irreconcilable with my conception of a God of love; the conviction that our material bodies are but garments in which we are clothed for a temporary purpose, and bearing no more permanent relation to us than the husk bears to the corn, or the shell to the walnut, or than the type to the thoughts I am here trying to express with them; that death, so far from being an interruption to man's life, is rather a ministry unto life, and as necessary a step in it as cutting our teeth or any other process of development; that through its gates we are admitted into a state of existence in which our faculties will be emancipated from the restrictions of sense, and their embryonic capacities indefinitely increased in proportions but faintly represented by the growth of the giant oak from the embryonic acorn; that the spiritual life is but a con-

is signified the *proprium,* from this circumstance, that it was the woman who deceived; for nothing ever deceives man but the *proprium,* or what is the same, the love of self and of the world."

tinuation of our life on earth, and that heaven consists
of a practically unlimited gratification of those prevailing loves in harmony with Divine laws, which the dying
carry with them; that hell consists of an equally free
indulgence of the prevailing lusts and passions not in
harmony with the Divine order, which the dying carry
with them; that, whether in heaven or in hell, we have
what in life we have prepared ourselves most to enjoy,
and that an abode in heaven would be as full of torture
to one without heavenly affections, as hell would be to
one with such affections; and, finally, that God's mercy
or love, which "is over all His works," is manifested
just as unceasingly, and just as bountifully, towards
those whose loves have attracted them to the one place,
as to those whose loves have attracted them to the other; that He is always in the effort to give to every
one, whether regenerate or unregenerate, all the happiness such person is capable of receiving. This I found,
when I had divested myself of some of the prejudices
in which I had been educated, was the teaching of the
Bible, and that the sensuous heaven and hell of the pop-
ular theology was simply a vulgar expression of our
most corrupt and selfish instincts.

Sixth. That God's infinite love is bestowed as constantly upon the greatest sinner as upon the greatest
saint, is manifested as fully in what we regard as tribulations or calamities as in what, in the worldly sense, we
regard as blessings, as prosperity, as triumphs. That so
far from having a penal purpose, our tribulations are
merciful warnings that we are violating some of the
laws of our being, the observance of which is indis-
pensable to our supreme happiness and are permitted

64

only to incite us to trace our errors to their hiding places and to correct them.

Seventh. In confessing what I am in the habit of regarding as the most conspicuous of my obligations, under Providence, to Swedenborg, I reserve for the last, the one without which I possibly should never have had the grace to understand or appropriate those already enumerated, and one which I regard as by far the most important contribution made to the science of theology since the death of the Apostles. I refer to his disclosure of the correspondential language in which God has chosen to reveal Himself to man in His Word.

To aid in the comprehension of this doctrine of correspondence, to which I attach such value, I must pause for a little to consider what sort of a book we should expect the Bible to be; how the Word of God must have been written to serve as a lamp to the feet and a light to the path of the children of men; in what sort of language infinite truth could be made intelligible to finite beings; and, finally, in what respect such a Book should necessarily differ from secular literature.

Obviously, God's Word could not be addressed exclusively to any particular stage of intellectual maturity, for "His tender mercies are over all His works." It necessarily had to be written for the instruction of the young, as well as of the aged; for the weak, as well as for the strong; for the ignorant, as well as for the learned; for the idolater, as well as for the monotheist. It had, also, to be written not for any particular nation, nor for any particular generation; no more for the saint than the savage, for the Jew than for the Gentile.

Neither can we conceive of such a Book being written for any particular era or stage of civilization. On the contrary, such a message had to be suited to the intelligence and spiritual perceptions of every generation, of every nation, of every era, in every age and stage of civilization, for God is no respecter of persons. Nor is that all. It had to be adapted to all the changes and spiritual fluctuations to which every human soul ever has been or ever can be subject; its lessons adapted to every possible stage in the process of every human being's spiritual regeneration or degeneration. It is not possible to conceive of God the Infinite and Eternal giving His preference to any nation or tribe, or providing less carefully for one period of our lives than for another, for the old than for the young, for the mature than the immature—for the rich than for the poor, for the learned than for the ignorant, for the saint than for the savage. A book of instructions essential to salvation, addressed to any peculiar people or tribe, or to the people of any particular epoch, age, worldly or spiritual condition, would necessarily absolve all outside of those categories respectively, from any culpability or responsibility for disregarding those instructions, and would imply limitations of God's interest in the salvation of His creatures, which would be wholly inconsistent with the essential attributes of the Divine Nature.

Nor is this all. The inferiority of all creatures to the Creator is infinite. The angels are as much His creatures as any of their ancestors in the heavens or their descendants on earth, and therefore must be presumed to have as much to learn from the teachings of Infinite Wisdom in the spiritual world, as when they dwelt

66

among men in the flesh; indeed, more, for they may be assumed to be more enlightened, and capable of receiving more. The Book, therefore, which professes to be the Word of God, and a guide in the ways of salvation, should express truths unconditionally adapted to the spiritual needs of all His creatures, at all times, under all circumstances, from the beginning and to all eternity. Any other conception of God's Word to His creatures could not be consistent with the essential attributes of Divinity.

It is plain that each of these conditions differentiates such a book profoundly from any imaginable human composition. Swedenborg assures us, and I think demonstrates, that in the Bible—the Books*—we have God's Word precisely so conditioned and differentiated from all other books. What, then, are the structural differences between the Word and all other human compositions, which gives such limitless scope to its teachings?

The natural world in which we live, with all its phenomena, is a world of effects. The causes of such effects, as I have already stated, lie far back in the will, or more properly speaking, in the spiritual world. All the phenomena of life, by which I mean everything of which we take cognizance by or through the senses, are but the sensual manifestations or effects of spiritual causes, the action of some will, without which action

* The Greek word *Biblia*, signifying the Books, is plural, and passed into the Latin as *Biblia,* which at first was a neuter plural. It gradually passed over into a feminine singular because of the habit of regarding the Scriptures as one work. All the modern translations have followed the usage of the old Church. Did they and the late Revisers do so, erring?

they could not have been manifested. Phenomena are representations of the will or purpose which begat them. There must, therefore, be not only a relation but a correspondence between every phenomenon, which is material, and its parent will. This correspondence has been aptly compared to the relation of speech to thought; of the printed page to the ideas it expresses. Every material object and phenomenon expresses so precisely the motive or will of which it was begotten, that a person as competent to read the language of all phenomena as he is to read the books written in his native tongue, would in one, as in the other, think only of the idea, motive, or will it expressed, rarely ever of the phenomenon or type by which the parent idea was made intelligible to him through the senses. When we see a smile on the face of a friend, or a tear in his eye, our mind does not dwell upon the muscular change in the one case, nor upon the fountain in the other, but upon the pleasant affection or tender sympathy of which they are the natural interpreters. The smile or the tear correspond with the emotion which they manifest, though neither has anything to do with producing the emotion, or has any consciousness of it. The human face reveals to the most careless observer well-defined qualities of character, and it is those qualities only, whether correctly or incorrectly divined, that we commonly carry in our memories. One person we say is cunning; another, open and frank; a third, vain; a fourth, cruel, and so on. The features represent or correspond with the several qualities of cunning, frankness, vanity, and cruelty, which have been indulged in to a greater or

68

less excess. This idea is happily expressed in a familiar couplet of the "Faery Queen"— .

> "For of the Soul the bodie form doth take,
> For Soul is forme and doth the bodie make."

There is nothing, there can be nothing, therefore, in the natural world which does not represent something in the spiritual world, or which has not there something with which it corresponds. The natural world, its activities and phenomena, are the language of God: the tones or utterances of infinitude adapted to the comprehension of mortal man, and when we read in the Word, of the deluge, of the ark, of mountains and rivers, of lambs, wolves, wars, honey, frankincense, myrrh, or of any other natural objects or phenomena, we are reading vital truths, disguised in a language suited to every possible stage of spiritual enlightenment. This visible world is in fact, the thought of God expressed in a language adapted to the intelligence and edification of all its inhabitants, in every possible stage of spiritual development.

"All nature, and each individual thing in nature," says Swedenborg, "has its spiritual correspondence; and, in like manner, each and all things in the human body. But hitherto it has been unknown what correspondence is. Yet it was very well known in the most ancient times; for to those who then lived the knowledge of correspondence was the knowledge of knowledges, and was so universal that all their books and manuscripts were written by correspondence. The Book of Job, which is a book of the Ancient Church, is full of correspondences. The hieroglyphics of the Egyptians, and the fabulous stories of highest anti-

69

quity, were nothing else. Also, the tabernacle with all things therein as well as their feasts,—such as the feast of unleavened bread, the feast of tabernacles, the feast of first-fruits;—and the priesthood of Aaron and the Levites, and their garments of holiness; and besides these, all their statutes and judgments, which related to their worship and life, were correspondences. Now, since Divine things present themselves in the world by correspondences, therefore the Word was written by pure correspondences. For the same reason the Lord, as He spake from the Divine spake by correspondences; for whatever is from the Divine descends into such things in nature as correspond to the Divine, and which then conceal things Divine, which are called celestial and spiritual, in their bosom."

"Without the spiritual sense," says he in another place, "no one could know why the prophet Jeremiah was commanded to buy himself a girdle and put it on his loins, and not to draw it through the waters, but to hide it in the hole of a rock by the Euphrates (Jer. xiii. 1-7), or why the prophet Isaiah was commanded to loose the sackcloth from off his loins and put off the shoe from off his foot, and to go naked and barefoot three years (Isaiah xx. 2, 3); or why the prophet Ezekiel was commanded to pass a razor upon his head and upon his beard, and afterwards to divide them [the hairs] and burn a third part in the midst of the city, smite a third part with the sword, scatter a third part in the wind, and bind a little of them in his skirts, and at last to cast them into the midst of the fire (Ezek. vi. 4); or why the same prophet was commanded to lie upon his left side three hundred and ninety days, and upon his right side forty days; and to make him a cake of wheat and barley and millet and fitches, with cow's dung, and eat it, and in the mean time to raise a rampart and a mound against Jerusalem and besiege it (Ezek. iv. 1-5) ; or why the prophet Hosea was twice commanded to take to himself a harlot to wife (Hosea i. 2-9, iii. 2, 3) ; and many such things. Moreover, who, without the spiritual sense, would know what is signified by all things belonging to the tabernacle,—by the ark, the mercy-seat, the cherubim, the candle-stick, the altar of incense, the bread of faces on the table, and its veils and curtains? Or who, without the spiritual sense, would know what is signified by Aaron's garments of holiness,—by his coat, his cloak, his ephod, the Urim and Thummim, the mitre and other things? Who, without the spiritual sense, would know what is signified by all the things which were enjoined concerning burnt-offerings, sacrifices, meat-offerings and drink-offerings? Concerning Sabbaths also, and feasts? *The truth is that not the least thing of these was enjoined which did not signify something relating to the Lord, to heaven and to the church.* From these few examples it may be clearly seen that there is a spiritual sense in each and all the particulars of the Word."

The Book of Genesis, from its beginning to the call of Abram (chapters i.-xi.), adds Swedenborg, was not written by Moses, but is a fragment of an older Scripture; neither are those early chapters matter-of-fact history, but compositions, in the form of history, symbolical of things celestial and spiritual.

"They who do not think beyond the sense of the letter, cannot believe otherwise than that the Creation described in the first and second chapters of Genesis means the creation of the universe; and that within six days, heaven and earth and sea, and things therein, and men in the likeness of God, were created; but who, if he ponder deeply, cannot see, that the creation of the universe is not there meant? Common-sense might teach that the operations there described were impossible; as, that there were days, and light and darkness, and green herbs and fruitful trees, be-fore the appearance of the sun and moon. Similar difficulties follow, which are scarcely credited by any one who thinks interiorly: as, that the woman was built from the rib of the man; that two trees were set in Paradise, and the fruit of one forbidden to be eaten; that the serpent discoursed with the wife of the man, who was the wisest of mortals, and deceived them both; and the universal human race was on that account condemned to hell.

"Nevertheless it is to be noted, that all things in that story, even to the smallest iota, are divine, and contain in them arcana, which before the angels in the heavens are manifest as in a clear day."

Swedenborg avers that in their highest state of ex-cellence, in the Church before the flood, men had an intuitive perception of the correspondences that uni-versally exist in nature, so that their language was the language of nature, that is, of correspondences; and that consequently the rites of the Church became cor-respondential, and representative of heavenly things; but that in time men became sensual and lost their per-ception of correspondences, and the rites of the Church lost, in their minds, their representative character. In observing the rites irrespective of the spiritual things they represented, they at length became idolatrous.

That there was a more ancient revelation than ours, as Swedenborg affirms, is proved by abundant allu-sions to them in our Word: for example *The Book of the Wars of Jehovah* is cited in Numbers xxi. 14 and Joshua x. 13; the *Book of Jasher* is cited in II Samuel

i. 18; *The Proverbial Enunciations* are cited in Numbers xxi. 27, 30. Besides there were the *Sayings of the Seers,* II Chronicles xxxiii. 19, *The Prophecy of Aijah,* cited in II Chronicles ix. 29, and *The Book of Nathan,* cited I Chronicles xxix. 29.

All these records were written in the language of correspondence or symbolically, and if they had survived would not be intelligible except to those to whom the language of correspondence had been disclosed, and so far only as it had been disclosed. The scraps of them which we find in the Bible are remnants only of sacred books far older than any script now extant, and which contained the wisdom suited to a people far more simple, unselfish and intuitively wise than any of whom history has preserved any record. To recover this lost knowledge of correspondences, Swedenborg claims that a new revelation from the Lord was necessary; that, for reasons which he assigns, he was selected as the medium through which that revelation was to be made,—at the time, and at the earliest time, when the world was prepared to receive and profit by it; just as the apostles, Moses and the prophets, were severally and at different periods of human history, selected for their respective offices. Swedenborg's own testimony upon this subject, already cited, is very remarkable. Nor did he shrink from reasserting his Divine commission on all suitable occasions.

He says in the *True Christian Religion,* No. 1779:

I testify in truth that the Lord manifested Himself to me His servant, and sent me to this office; and that afterwards He opened the sight of my spirit and so intromitted me into the spiritual world, and has

73

granted me to see the heavens and the hells, and also to converse with angels and spirits, and this now continually for many years; likewise that from the first day of that calling I have not received anything whatever relating to the doctrines of that Church from any angel, but from the Lord alone while I was reading the Word.

Again, in the *Apocalypse Explained,* No. 1183, he says:

It has been given me to perceive distinctly what comes from the Lord and what from angels; what has come from the Lord has been written, and what from the angels has not been written.

In his *Invitation to the New Church* he says also:

The things related by me are not miracles, but are proofs that for certain ends I have been introduced by the Lord into the spiritual world.

The chief results of these communications or revelations were recorded in three distinct works.

The first, entitled *Arcana Cœlestia,** appeared in eight quarto volumes, between the years 1749 and 1756, at the rate of about one volume a year, and was consecrated to an exposition of the internal or spiritual sense of the books of Genesis and Exodus. Each sentence is taken up in its order, and its spiritual import laid open; for Swedenborg maintained that "there is not an iota or apex or little twirl of the Hebrew letters which does not involve something Divine." "This," he says, "has been shown to me from heaven; but I know it transcends belief."†

* *Arcana Cœlestia quæ in Scriptura Sacra, seu in Verbo Domini sunt, detecta; una cum mirabilius, quæ visa sunt in Mundi Spirituum et cœlo Angelorum.*

† *Arc. Cœlestia,* No. 4049.

Second. The *Apocalypse Revealed,* wherein are uncovered the mysteries there foretold which have hitherto remained concealed.*

Third. The *Apocalypse Explained,* wherein are disclosed the mysteries there foretold, which have hitherto remained concealed.† The former is more summary, and the latter a more extended work, involving incidentally an exposition of a very considerable part of the rest of the Word.

"This year," says Swedenborg in a letter to his friend Oetinger, writing from Stockholm, Sept. 23, 1766, "there has been published the *Apocalypsis Revelata,* which was promised in the treatise on *The Last Judgment,* and from which it may be clearly seen that I converse with angels; for not the smallest verse in the Apocalypse can be understood without revelation. Who can help seeing that by the New Jerusalem a New Church is meant, and that its doctrines can only be revealed by the Lord,—because they are described there by merely typical things, *i. e.,* by correspondences; and likewise that these can be published to the world only by means of some one to whom the revelation has been granted? I can solemnly bear witness that the Lord Himself appeared to me, and that He sent me to do that which I am now doing; and that for this purpose He has opened the interiors of my mind, which are those of my spirit, so that I can see the things which are in the spiritual world, and hear those who are there; which

* *Apocalypsis Revelata in qua deteguntur arcana quæ ibi prædicta sunt, et hactenus recondita latuerunt.* Amsterdam, 1766, 4to, pp. 629.

† *Apocalypsis Explicata secundum sensum spiritualem ubi revelantur arcana quæ ibi prædicta et hactenus recondita fuerent ex operibus posthumis Emanuelis Swedenborgii.* Londoni, in 4 vols., 4to, vol. 1, 1785; vol. 2, 1786; vol. 3, 1788; vol. 4, 1789.

[privilege] I have had now for twenty-two years. The mere bearing witness, however, does not suffice at the present day to convince men of this; but any one of a sound understanding may be confirmed by the testimony of my writings, and especially by the *Apocalypsis Revelata*. Who has heretofore known anything about the spiritual sense of the Word; and about the spiritual world, or heaven and hell; or about man's life after death? Should these, and many other things, be perpetually hidden from Christians? They have now for the first time been disclosed for the sake of the New Church, which is the New Jerusalem, that they [its members] may know them; others indeed shall also know them, who yet do not know them on account of their unbelief."

Swedenborg does not profess to give all the internal meaning of which the Word is the repository. So far from it, he represents the Word to be infinite; to contain even profounder depths of wisdom than can be expressed in the language of men; adapted, by successive unfoldings, to the angels of all the heavens,—to the highest state of intelligence that finite minds can ever, to all eternity, attain; and extending upwards even to God Himself, as the rays of light extend to the sun. In other words, that it is in the true sense of the term Divine, and therefore infinite. Hence the necessity that the natural language of the Bible should be that of correspondences, capable of involving these hidden things, and so of being adapted to every spiritual state of men on earth and in the heavens. Swedenborg would therefore claim that the highest evidence of the divine authority of the Bible is to be found in the marvellous light of the manifold but harmonious meanings inhabiting its letter, which the devout and reverent-minded may find revealed through the knowledge of its correspondences now again made known. He teaches, too, that nature is a similar treasury of Divine wisdom, and capable of similar unfoldings,—a vast, continuous series of cause and effect within cause and effect, extending up to God Himself. So that His revealed or written Word and His Word in Nature alike descend from Him, and lead up to Him, who is the inmost and animating soul of both; not a mere undefined pervading influence, but a Divine Personal God,—an infinitely glorious Divine Man, the great Archetype, of which man was created the finite image.

"Without such a living principle," he says, "the Word as to the letter is dead. For it is with the Word as it is with man, who, as all Christians are taught to believe, consists of two parts, an external and an internal. The external man separate from the internal is the body, which in such a state of separation is dead; but the internal is that which lives and causes the external to live. The internal man is the soul; and thus the Word, as to the letter alone, is like a body without a soul."

Have we not here an explanation and a solution of the difficulties which furnish the pretexts of Higher Criticism so called, to distract the various religious societies of Christendom and undermine the faith of multitudes in the Bible, and in the God of Abraham and of Isaac and of Jacob? What else is it but the "dreary literalism" in which, according to a former bishop of New York, the Bible has been for many years walled up, or according to Swedenborg, the Bible as a body without a soul, which is the same thing? *

VII

THERE probably has never been a line written that has unsettled the faith of so many in the Divine origin and authority of the Bible, as the opening sentence of that sacred volume:

In the *beginning* God created the heavens and the earth.

Assuming, as the Christian world with practical unanimity has done, that the Mosaic chronology dates from this "beginning" it holds to this day that our world is about 6,000 years old, while science has demonstrated that 600,000 years is much nearer to the truth. *Falsus in uno falsus in omnibus* is a doctrine as conclusive in ecclesiastical as in civil law, and the Agnostic exclaims,

---

* For the information of those to whom Swedenborg is comparatively a stranger, and this unhappily includes most of those who might derive the greatest advantage from an acquaintance with his writings—the "Orthodox Clergy"—they will find, in the Appendix, a list of the Theological writings of Swedenborg and the dates of their composition embracing over forty distinct works in nearly half as many volumes. Of these several works, a concordance has been published in which a reference to every passage in them with a brief extract is given, arranged in alphabetical order, and ranging in length from a single line to many pages. This gigantic work, as a monument of patient intellectual industry, does not suffer by a comparison with the most laborious achievements of the Benedictine monks. It has occupied the compiler, editor and translator, the Rev. John Faulkner Potts, over twenty years, and contains more words than the Century Dictionary. I do not know where to look in all the secular literature of the world for another publication so abounding in luminous suggestions touching the loftiest themes of human concern.

"How absurd to ascribe divine authority to a book that begins with what appears to be either a gross blunder or a falsehood!"

Swedenborg tells us that this first chapter of Genesis, which is commonly supposed to treat only of the creation of the world, and of the Garden of Eden called Paradise, and of Adam as the first created man, really treats of the second birth or new creation of man, that is, his regeneration, and that the six days of creation represent so many successive stages of his regeneration. The first stage is that which is referred to as the "beginning," and includes both the state of infancy and the state immediately preceding regeneration. This is called vacuity, emptiness and darkness, and the first movement is the Spirit of God moving upon the face of the waters. "The beginning," he says, "implies the first time when man is regenerating, for then he is born anew and receives life, hence regeneration, which signifies a new creation."

"The people which *shall be created* shall praise the Lord." Psalm cii. 18.

"Thou sendest forth thy Spirit, *they are created.*" Psalm civ. 30.

Thus "the beginning," referred to in the first verse of Genesis, does not refer to any particular epoch in time, but is applicable to every regenerating soul in all time. "Good," says Swedenborg, "has life in itself, because it is from the Lord, who is life itself." In the life which is from the Lord there is wisdom and intelligence, for to receive good from the Lord, and thence to will good, is wisdom, and to receive truth from the Lord, and thence to believe truth is intelligence, and they who have this

79

wisdom and intelligence have life, and whereas happiness is adjoined to such life, eternal happiness is also what is signified by life." The antithesis to this, the real life, is that death which follows the extinction of spiritual life. It is the birth and development of the real life in this sense, with which human science has found itself hitherto so incompetent to cope. And it is difficult to see how any one who is a seeker for truth, and not merely for a confirmation of preconceived opinion, can read Swedenborg's exegesis of it without approving of his interpretation and without finding any difficulties of a scientific character by which he may have been disturbed, completely dispelled; without finding in it "the history of his own life in its progress from darkness, desolation and chaos to the glory, beauty and peace of an endless Sabbath."

I am here tempted to quote a very striking passage on this very subject from the writings of William Law to show how one of the most eminent divines of the English Established Church reached the same conclusion as Swedenborg, so far as to consider the word "beginning," in the first chapter of Genesis, to refer to a state and not to a period in time. And curiously enough he published this conclusion about twenty years after the appearance of Swedenborg's commentary, in a paper entitled "An Appeal to all that doubt or disbelieve the truths of the Gospel, whether they be Deists, Arians, Socinians or Nominal Christians," etc.*

* This appeal appeared in 1768. The first volume of the *Arcana Cœlestia,* containing Swedenborg's commentary upon the first chapter of Genesis, was published in 1749. It is known that Law was a subscriber for the *Arcana,* but neither in what is quoted here, nor in anything he ever published, is there any

Properly and strictly speaking, nothing can begin to be; The Beginning of everything is nothing more than its beginning to be in a *New State*. Thus *Time* itself does not begin to be, but Duration, which always was, began to be measured by the Earth's turning round, or the rising and setting of the Sun, and that is called the Beginning of Time, which is properly speaking, only the Beginning of the measure of Duration. Thus it is with all temporal Nature and all the Qualities and Powers of temporal Beings that live in it. No Quality or Power of Nature *then* began to be, but such Qualities and Powers as had been from all Eternity, began then to be in a *New State*. Ask what Time is; it is nothing else but something of Eternal Duration become finite, measurable and transitory. Ask what Fire, Light, Darkness, Air, Water and Earth are; they are and can be nothing else but some Eternal Things become gross, finite, measurable, divisible and transitory. For if there could be Fire that did not spring out of Eternal Fire, then there might be Time that did not come out of Eternity.

It is thus with every temporary thing and the qualities of it; it is not the beginning of Nothing, but only of a *New State* of something that existed before of Eternal Nature, and is nothing else but so much of Eternal Nature changed from its eternal to a temporal condition. Fire did not begin to be; Light did not begin to be; Water and Earth did not begin to be when this temporary World first appeared, but all these things came out of their eternal state into a lower, divided, compacted and transitory state. Hearing, Seeing, Tasting, Smelling, Feeling, did not then begin to be, when God first created the creatures of this World; they only came to be Qualities and Powers

direct allusion to Swedenborg by name or to his works. Law's practical works all betray an acquaintance, though hardly a familiarity, with his writings.

81

of a lower and more imperfect order of Beings than they had been before. Figures and their relations did not begin to be, when material circles, squares, etc., were first made, but these Figures and Relations began then to appear in a lower State than they had done before; and so it must be said of our temporal Nature and everything in it. It is only something of Eternal Nature separated, changed or created into a temporary state or condition.*

The undervaluation of the Bible is the infirmity of the flocks and the vice of the shepherds throughout Christendom. Both treat the Bible mostly as the savages treat the soil, harvesting and hunting only what grows spontaneously on the surface. They too rarely turn it up to see what wealth is stored up for them beneath. Both look with more or less suspicion or contempt upon those who explore and toil for the hidden wealth. This disposition is neither logical nor theological. No one can read the Bible, however superficially, without finding himself occasionally obliged to go beyond the literal to the spiritual meaning of its language to get any edification from it.

Solomon proposed to build a house for the *name* of the Lord (I Kings, v. 5); and every time we utter the Lord's prayer we say, "Hallowed be Thy Name.' How shall the literalist expound these words? What does a name need of a house? How does it occupy a house? What kind of a house can a name occupy? Farther on in the 9th Chapter of Kings, the Lord says, "I have hallowed this house which thou hast built to put my name there forever, and mine eyes and mine heart shall be

* William Law's Works, Vol. vi., p. 114.

there perpetually." The young and the very ignorant when they read these passages may suppose that in some way these statements are literally true; that the house was built for a name, and that God did somehow put His eyes and heart there. When, however, they begin to reflect, it dawns upon them that the name here referred to must signify something more than the numeral to which the soldier or prisoner answers at roll call. No educated clergyman would construe these words literally. They would generally treat it as figurative, or metaphorical, merely leaving the impression that another writer having occasion to record the same story might have employed quite different words and illustrations. In this way God's Word is treated as if it were subject to all the fluctuations and caprices of human speech, a treatment entirely irreconcilable with its Divine authenticity.

So when we pray the Father to give us our "daily bread," no inconsiderable portion of the Christian world regard this as simply a prayer that their daily recurring bodily appetite may be gratified, assuming that the word "bread" here is only a general term for any suitable nutriment for the body. But one can have read the Bible to very little purpose not to have discovered that the bread in this prayer signifies not only the kind of food that is essential to the growth and development of the body, but also of higher and more enduring life in man, in other words spiritual food; food suited to the nourishment of our spiritual life day by day.

Bread (from grain), says Swedenborg, in general corresponds to the affection of all good, because it supports life more than other things, and because all food is meant by it. On account of this correspondence the Lord is called the Bread of Life. "Thou feedest them with the bread of tears," says the Psalmist (Ps. lxxx. 5). "The virtuous woman," says Solomon, "looketh well to the ways of her household and eateth not the bread of idleness" (Prov., ch. xxxi. 27). It is obvious enough that in neither of the cases here cited is there any question of the nourishment of the body merely. Nor when Moses said to the Children of Israel, "Neither fear the people of the land, they are bread for us." The people of the land here referred to, are the lusts, the passions, the evil propensities of every human heart, and "he that overcometh them shall not be hurt of second death." "They shall eat of the bread of life." "He that overcometh shall sit with me in my throne." Such is the kind of bread that Moses promised to those of his followers who bravely pursued and overcame the enemies of their own households.

Again, when the Lord said to His disciples, "I am the Vine and ye are the branches," He was not teaching vegetable physiology nor talking poetry, as any one may see by noting the stations of dignity and consequence occupied by the vine and every product of the vine, as well as the "branch" in nearly every book of the Bible.

The prophet forecasts the birth of our Saviour in these words: "Behold a Virgin shall conceive and bear a Son, and shall call his name Immanuel. Butter and honey shall he eat, that he may know to refuse the evil and choose the good."*

What have butter and honey in their literal sense to do with our choice between good and evil? It is no irreverence, we hope, to say that if it has no other than

* Isaiah vii. 14.

84

the literal meaning it is nonsense; but as representing and corresponding with the faculty by which we love the good and eschew evil it is everything.

When we read in John that Jesus cured the blind man by anointing his eyes with His own spittle mingled with clay, it is our first impulse to ask why did He not prevent the man becoming blind, and why resort to such a process to cure him when He had but to say the word and the man's sight would have been restored? Obviously something more than blindness of the body was involved in this miracle, and something more than a simple eye ointment was employed in his cure. It is not until we observe how frequently "blindness" is used to express the absence of divine light that we see how perfectly our Saviour's remedy was adapted to the infirmity.

If some words in any one book of the Bible have a spiritual or interior meaning, why not in all of that book? Can a motive be conceived for giving a spiritual meaning to some word of a Divine message and not to all? Is not a discrimination equivalent to an impeachment of its Divine authorship?

Swedenborg tells us, as I have already remarked, that in the Most Ancient Church before the flood, the language of the world was entirely correspondential, and when natural phenomena were named they were but as words that express the spiritual idea with which they corresponded, the phenomena occupying no more of the speaker's thought or attention than the paper or letters of a book do of the thought or attention of its reader.

At the Deluge, the children of men had so far lost the correspondential language that the phenomena of nature had practically ceased to be intelligible to them;

85

they had become as a page of a book to a child who cannot read, who can spell out the characters, but having little or no suspicion of the thought those characters were intended to express.

It is perhaps the greatest, as it is the most nearly universal delusion of mankind to ascribe causality to physical phenomena; to suppose the events in nature, of which we take note through the senses, to be something more or other than a series of effects from the spiritual causes which they represent. True, the order and connexion of events and circumstances appear to us for wise reasons, which I will not interrupt this narrative to explain, to stand towards each other in the nature of cause and effect; but the harmony and order which we mistake for cause and effect are but the inevitable consequences of the order, connexion and succession of their spiritual causes, and of the Divine order reigning through the whole.

This correspondency, therefore, between the two worlds of spirit and of matter, of cause and effect, must be universal. It can admit of no exception. It does not consist in affixing certain abitrary meanings to certain objects, nor in the tracing of a metaphorical or poetical resemblance between a certain state of the mind and a certain event in nature, but it is the necessary link, the umbilical cord, which unites the spiritual world with its natural progeny, and in accordance with which the state of the human will and understanding are represented in the sensible appearances of space and time.

"We must not suffer the natural semblance of physical causes to affect our mental sight," says a profound student of Swedenborg's spiritual philosophy,

86

"for from physical causes there is but one step to the belief in accidental cause, or in the existence of a cause without an end or purpose. But he whose eye is spirtually enlightened will see that from the universality of the Divine Providence operating from ends through causes in effects, *there can be no such thing as accidents;* for those things which are falsely considered accidental, with all their consequences, have their causes as much in the spiritual world or state *as the words of language have their causes in the thoughts which they indicate;* or, as the expression of the countenance is an effect which unfolds and represents the state of the affections."*

"Wherever in the universe," says Swedenborg, "any object appears, it is a representative of the Lord's kingdom; so much so, that there is actually nothing in the atmospheric and starry universe, nothing in the earth and its three kingdoms, that does not, after its kind, represent. For in nature the whole, and every part of the whole, are ultimate images. From the Divine essence are celestial states of goodness, and from these, spiritual states of truth, and, from both of them conjointly, natural objects; and because all things, as well as each thing singly, subsist from the Divine essence—that is, continually exist from Him —and as all their derivatives must of necessity represent those states through which they become extant, therefore, it follows that the visible is nothing else but a theatre, representative of the Lord's kingdom, and this latter a theatre representative of the Lord Himself." †

"Throughout nature there is not a single thing which can exist unless it have a correspondency with

* The Science of Correspondence and other Spiritual Doctrine, etc., by Charles Augustus Tulk.
† *Arcana Cœlestia,* n. 3483.

87

the spiritual world, for without it, it would want a cause for its existence, and, consequently, for its subsistence also. For all things in nature are nothing else but effects, the causes of which are in the spiritual world, and the causes of these which are ends, in the interior heaven. *The effect cannot subsist unless the cause be continually in it, for the cause ceasing, the effect must cease also.* The effect considered in itself is nothing else but the cause, but so extrinsically clothed as to be subservient to the cause by enabling it to act in a lower sphere. What is here said of the effect in relation to its cause, is equally true of the cause in relation to its end. For a cause is nothing unless it exist from its cause which is the end; for without an end it is a cause devoid of order, and without order nothing can be effected."*

VIII

The Doctrine of Correspondences of which I have endeavoured to give the reader some notion—he must turn to Swedenborg's exegetical writings for an adequate comprehension of it—has been more or less recognized in all ages; we find traces of it in the literature of all nations. Saint Paul frequently refers to it; it was distinctly recognized by the Fathers.

Origen in his account of Sarah and Abimelech, of Isaac and Rebecca, and of the midwives of Egypt, says:

If any choose to understand this merely according to the letter, he ought to seek his hearers rather among the Jews than among Christians.

* *Arcana Cœlestia,* n. 5711.

The writings of the mystics owe pretty much all of whatever vitality they possessed to the spiritual significance they have discerned within the letter of the Word. During the interval between the Council of Nice and the illumination of Swedenborg, the Christian Church was engaged in struggles with the more or less barbarous elements of society with which it had to deal, elements to which the letter appealed more powerfully than its spirit. During this long interval, the Church was preoccupied first with the struggle between papal and secular sovereigns for supremacy, and later with the prelatical struggle which preceded and followed the Reformation. The triumph of Protestantism in Germany and England emancipated Science and led to a more careful study of the constitution and laws of nature, and not only prepared the Christian world, but compelled it to go to the Bible itself and not to councils nor hierarchies for a reconciliation of its sacred teachings with the equally sacred teachings of Nature. Swedenborg attended the lectures of Sir Isaac Newton, whose discoveries gave the first important and enduring impulse in Europe to the study of Natural Science, and whose theological writings also betrayed an intelligent discontent with the notions of the Trinity* then taught by the Established Church, circumstances both indicating him in a special sense, a providential precursor of Swedenborg.

Blaise Pascal, whose premature death deprived France of one of the most acute and brilliant intellects she has yet to boast of, and whose piety was not less

* "Newton's Historical Account of Two Notable Corruptions of the Scripture," addressed to John Locke.

extraordinary than his genius, came as near as any one not specially illuminated for that mission, in divining the structural principle of the Word as disclosed by Swedenborg.

His argument that it was written with an internal or spiritual, as well as with an external or natural sense, is original and striking, though he gives no evidence of possessing any exact knowledge of the science of correspondence, or of having any key to the precise spiritual significance of the natural phenomena referred to in the Word, except so far as their significance is disclosed in the Bible itself. He inferred an internal meaning as Columbus inferred a western route to the Indies. What that internal meaning was, he had of course only a conjectural knowledge.

In the sixteenth Article of his *Pensees* Pascal says:

> To prove both Testaments at once we have but to see if the prophecies of the one are accomplished in the other. To test the prophecies, it is necessary to understand them, for if we believe they have but a single sense, it is certain that the Messiah will not have come; but if they have a double sense (or a literal and a spiritual), it is certain that He will have come in Jesus Christ.

Farther on, and speaking of the literal inconsistencies of the Old Testament, he says:

> It is said that the law shall be changed;* that the sacrifice shall be changed†. That they shall be without a king,‡ without prince and without sacrifice; that he will make a new covenant. That the law shall be renewed; that the precepts they have received are not

* Jeremiah xxxi. 31.   † Daniel ix. 27.
‡ Hosea iii. 4.

good.* That their sacrifices are abominable.† That God has not asked them.‡

On the other hand, we are elsewhere told that the law shall endure forever, § that this covenant shall be eternal.‖ That the sacrifice shall be eternal,¶ that the sceptre shall never depart from them till the King eternal arrives.**

All these passages, are they to be accepted literally? No. Are they all to be taken figuratively? No; but as reality or figure. But the first excluding a literal interpretation, indicates that it is but figurative. All these things together can not be interpreted literally; they may all, however, be interpreted figuratively. Then they are not meant to be interpreted literally, but figuratively. *Agnus occisus est ab origine mundi.*††

A portrait imports absence and presence, what is pleasant and what is not pleasant. To know if the law and the sacrifices are to be regarded literally or figuratively we must see if the prophets in speaking of these matters rested their view and thought in the letter so as not to see but this ancient covenant, or if they saw something more of which it was but the picture; for in a portrait one sees the thing figured. For this purpose it is only necessary to study what they say.

When they say the covenant shall be eternal, do they mean to speak of a covenant which shall be changed, and so of the sacrifices?

The figure has two meanings. When one takes up an important letter where he finds a clear meaning,

* Ezekiel xx. 25, 31.　　　† Isaiah i. 13.
‡ Hosea vi. 6.　　　§ Baruch iv. 1.
‖ Genesis xvii. 13, 19.　　　¶ Jeremiah xxx. 18.
** Genesis xlix. 10.
†† These words of the Apocalypse xiii. 8, respond to the thought of Pascal, that the sacrifice of the Jews pre-figured the eternal sacrifice, that of Jesus Christ.

but wherein nevertheless it is stated that the sense is veiled and obscured, that it is concealed so that he shall see this letter without seeing it, and shall understand it without understanding it, what ought he to conclude, if not that it is a figure with a double meaning, more especially when he encounters manifest contradictions in the literal sense? How highly, then, ought we to esteem those who uncover this figure and reveal to us its concealed meaning, especially when the doctrines they derive from it are altogether natural and clear. It is that which Jesus Christ and the apostles have done. He has removed the seal, He has lifted the veil, He has uncovered the spirit. We are thus taught that the enemies of man are his passions, that the Redeemer should be spiritual, that He should come to us twice, once as a man of sorrows to humiliate the proud, the second time in glory to raise the humble; that Jesus Christ should be God and man. The prophets have said plainly that Israel should always be loved of God, and that the law should be eternal. And they have also said that their meaning would not be understood, that it was veiled."

Since Pascal's time the necessity of looking beyond the letter of the Word for the means of reconciling its teachings with the revelations of modern science has been extensively recognized by many of the most prominent and influential members of the "Orthodox Church."

"You are to observe," says William Law, in his discourse on *The Spirit of Love,* "that body begins not from itself, but is all that it is, whether pure or impure; has all that it has, whether of light or darkness, and works all that it works, whether of good or evil, merely from spirit. For nothing, my friend, acts in the whole universe of things but spirit alone.

And the state, condition and degree of every spirit is only and solely opened by the state, form, condition and qualities of the body that belongs to it, *for the body can have no nature, form, condition or quality, but that which the spirit that brings it forth gives to it.*"*

Later, in the same paper,† Law says:

"And now, gentlemen, you may easily apprehend how and why a God in whose holy Deity no spark of wrath or partiality can possibly arise, but who is, from eternity to eternity, only following forth in love, goodness and blessing to everything capable of it, could yet say of the children before they were born or had done either good or evil. 'Jacob have I loved, and Esau have I hated.' It is because Esau signifies the earthly, beastly nature that came from sin, and Jacob signifies the incorruptible seed of the Word that is to overcome Esau and change his mortal into immortality."

John Keble, now most widely known as the author of *The Christian Year,* in No. 89 of *Tracts of the Times,* the purpose of which was to vindicate the fathers of the Church from the supposed stigma attached to them on account of their alleged mysticism, expressed himself in language which would scarcely have been used by any one not more or less imbued with the views if not the teachings of Swedenborg, in regard to the structural principle of the Word.

"The Scriptures deal largely in symbolical language taken from natural objects. The chosen vehicle for the most direct divine communication has always been that form of speech which most readily adopts and in-

* The Works of William Law, Vol. viii., p. 22.
† P. 168.

vites such imagery, viz., the poetical. Is there not something very striking to a thoughtful, reverential mind, in the simple fact of symbolic language occurring in Scripture at all? That is, when truths *Scriptural* are represented in Scripture by visible and sensible imagery. Consider what this really comes to. The author of Scripture is the author of Nature. He made His creatures what they are, upholds them in their being, modifies it at His will, knows all their secret relations, associations and properties. We know not how much there may be far beyond metaphor and similitude, in His using the name of any one of His creatures in a translated sense, to shadow out something invisible. But thus far we may seem to understand, that the object thus spoken of by Him, is so far taken out of the number of ordinary figures of speech and resources of language, and partakes henceforth of the nature of a type.

"The text 'The invisible things from the creation of the world are clearly seen, being understood by the things that are made,' lays down a principle or canon of mystical interpretation for the works of nature. It is the characteristic tendency of poetical minds to make the world of sense, from beginning to end, symbolical of the absent and unseen; and poetry was the ordained vehicle of revelation, till God was made manifest in the flesh."

Those who are familiar with Keble's *Christian Year* cannot fail to have been struck with the following impressive lines, in which the Doctrine of Correspondence between the Natural and Spiritual Worlds is distinctly recognized:

> There is a Book, who runs may read,
>   Which heavenly truth imparts;
> And all the lore its scholars need,
>   Pure eyes and Christian hearts.

The works of God above, below,
  Within us and around,
Are pages in that Book, to shew
  How God Himself is found.

    *   *   *   *   *

The worlds are airs; 'tis only sin
  Forbids us to descry
The mystic heaven and earth within,
  Plain as the sea and sky.

Thou who has given me eyes to see,
  And love this sight so fair;
Give me a heart to find out Thee,
  And read Thee everywhere.

Few men differ more widely in their general tone of
thought than Keble and the late Charles Kingsley, and
yet Kingsley like Keble appears to have been quite as
deeply impressed with the mysterious relations between
the Natural and Spiritual, or the visible and the invisible
worlds. In fact, he went beyond Keble in the extent to
which he recognized the spiritual language of nature.

"The great Mysticism," he says, "is the belief
which is becoming every day stronger with me, that
all symmetrical objects, aye, and perhaps all forms,
colors and scents which show organization or arrangement, are types of some spiritual truth or existence of a grade between the symbolical and the mystic
type. Everything seems to be full of God's reflex if
we could but see it. * * The visible world is in
some mysterious way a pattern or symbol of the invisible one; its physical laws are the analogues of the
spiritual laws of the eternal world."*

In a review of Vaughan's Hours with the Mystics,
Kingsley says again:

* Life of Kingsley, i. 77.

95

"The works of God in creation and providence, besides their uses in this life, appeared to the old writers
as so many intended tokens from the Almighty to as-
sure us of some spiritual fact or other which it con-
cerns us to know."

How strange it seems for a man of as wide reading
as Kingsley, to be groping about in the dark for the elements of a body of truth, which a century before Swedenborg had unfolded as fully and as clearly as the prin-
ciples of any modern science.

We do not realize how large a proportion of our
familiar speech depends for its excellence, by which I
mean its intelligibility, upon what we suppose to be the
relations and inter-dependence of nature and thought.
When we talk of "borrowing trouble," of the "fluctuations of fortune," the "milk of human kindness," of "a
hard head," "the scythe of Time," "an elevated character," "the frosts of age," "rosemary for remembrance,"
"a sweet face," "refined taste," or when we say of a
man that he is "true as steel," "cold as ice," "blind
to his true interests," "deaf to reason," that he has "a
voice of silver," "a face of brass," etc., we are more or
less rudely interpreting the language and lessons of
nature.

It is the great weakness of modern science that its
students do mostly limit their investigations to phenomena—that is, to facts cognizable by the senses—never
allowing themselves to look beyond the phenomena for
the Divine purpose of which they are the offspring. Instead of looking up from nature to nature's God, to as-
certain the will or motive which must have preceded the

96

phenomena, and inhabits them, they limit their inquiries to the purely phenomenal relations of nature.

The man who did not consider whether the hand extended to him by an acquaintance was intended as a salutation or a blow, would be classed as an idiot; and yet does the modern scientist work upon any higher plane than this idiot? He will allow himself to know and name all the letters on the printed page of nature, and there he stops. He does not attempt to translate and understand the higher lessons that page was intended to teach. Hence it is, perhaps, that the world is so little indebted to the devotees of natural science for ethical or religious truths, the only truths which in the long run are of any value, and the very truths which natural phenomena were specially intended to impart to us. The time must come when no one will be regarded as a philosopher, however familiar he may be with the phenomena of nature, or eminent as an experimentalist, unless he looks beyond physical to spiritual causes, and does what in him lies to put his fingers upon the chords of Divine harmony which connect every thing and event in nature with their Author.

One reason, perhaps the only reason, why poetry and poets have always enjoyed a larger measure of worldly esteem than scientists of the same relative rank, may fairly be attributed to the fact that all genuine poetry depends largely for its charm upon its success in divining the thoughts which lie concealed in nature as the statue is concealed in the block of native marble. Is it not the *conatus* of every true poet to decipher the spiritual truths which are expressed in the phenomenal world, and which the Master has been pleased to adapt es-

97

pecially to our earthly limitations? May not the merit of all, or at least of the highest order of poetry, be traced to the skill of the poet in drawing illustrations of abstract truth from natural objects? Let us turn to the pages of the first of English poets to see whether there is anything chimerical in this view. In each of the following passages it will be found that natural objects stand for, represent, correspond with and express some abstract idea, thought or sentiment of which the object itself could of course have had no conception; derive from what is material somewhat that is spiritual and for that purpose only is the material alluded to.

My salad days
When I was green in judgment.
—*Antony and Cleopatra, Act I., Sc.* 5.

But O, how bitter a thing it is to look into happiness through another man's eyes.—*As You Like It, Act V., Sc.* 2.

Thou art thy mother's glass, and she in thee
Calls back the lovely April of her prime;
So thou through windows of thine age shalt see,
Despite of wrinkles, this thy golden time.—*Sonnet III.*

Our life, exempt from public haunt,
Finds tongues in trees, books in the running brooks,
Sermons in stones, and good in everything.
—*As You like It, Act II., Sc.* 1.

Smooth runs the water where the brook is deep.
—*Second part of Henry VI., Act III., Sc.* 1.

Out of the nettle danger, we pluck this flower safety.
—*First part of Henry VI., Act II., Sc.* 3.

She was the sweet marjoram of the salad, or rather the herb of grace.—*All's Well that Ends Well, Act IV., Sc.* 5.

Time hath, my lord, a wallet at his back,
Wherein he puts alms for oblivion,
A great-sized monster of ingratitude.
—*Troilus and Cressida, Act III., Sc.* 3.

98

O Father Abbot,
An old man, broken with the storms of state,
Is come to lay his weary bones among ye;
Give him a little earth for charity.
                    —*Henry VIII., Act IV., Sc. 2.*

Death lies on her like an untimely frost
Upon the sweetest flower of the field.
                    —*Romeo and Juliet, Act IV., Sc. 5.*

Sweet flowers are slow and weeds make haste.
                    —*Richard III., Act II., Sc. 4.*

How poor are they that have no patience!
What wound did ever heal but by degrees?
                    —*Othello, Act II., Sc. 3.*

'Tis better to be lowly born
And range with humble livers in content,
Than to be perked up in a glistering grief
And wear a golden sorrow.—*Henry VIII., Act II., Sc. 3.*

How far that little candle throws his beams!
So shines a good deed in a naughty world.
                    —*Merchant of Venice, Act V., Sc. 1.*

Those friends thou hast and their adoption tried,
Grapple them to thy soul with hoops of steel.
                    —*Hamlet, Act I., Sc. 3.*

Let's carry with us ears and eyes for the time,
But hearts for the event.—*Coriolanus, Act II., Sc. 1.*

Why, what's the matter,
That you have such a February face,
So full of frost, of storm and cloudiness?
                    —*Much Ado About Nothing, Act V., Sc. 3.*

Truth hath a quiet breast.—*Richard II., Act I., Sc. 3.*

The expectancy and rose of this fair state.
                    —*Hamlet, Act III., Sc. 1.*

The fire of the flint shows not till it be struck.
                    —*Timon of Athens, Act I., Sc. 1.*

Haply I think on thee, and then my state,
Like to the lark at break of day arising,
From sullen earth, sings hymns at heaven's gate.
                    —*Sonnet XXIX.*

99

O two such silver currents, when they join,
Do glorify the banks that bound them in.
                    —*King John, Act II., Sc.* 1.

Nothing 'gainst time's scythe can make defence.
                              —*Sonnet XII.*

When the sea was calm all boats alike
Showed mastership in floating.—*Coriolanus, Act IV., Sc.* 1.

God be praised, that to believing souls
Gives light in darkness, comfort in despair.
                    —*Second part Henry VI., Act II., Sc.* 1.

The strawberry grows underneath the nettle.
                    —*Henry V., Act I., Sc.* 2.

My words fly up, my thoughts remain below:
Words without thoughts never to heaven go.
                    —*Hamlet, Act III., Sc.* 3.

I to the world am like a drop of water
That in the ocean seeks another drop.

'Tis in ourselves that we are thus or thus. Our bodies are
our gardens, to the which our wills are gardeners; so that if
we will plant nettles, or sow lettuce, set hyssop and weed up
thyme....have it sterile with idleness or manured with industry, why, the power and corrigible authority of this lies in
our wills.—*Othello, Act I., Sc.* 3.

If thou art rich, thou art poor,
For like an ass whose back with ingots bows,
Thou bear'st thy heavy burden but a journey,
And death unloads thee.
                    —*Measure for Measure, Act III., Sc.* 1.

It may be that in no single instance that we have
cited has Shakespeare discerned the true spiritual correspondence between his thought and the natural phenomena with which he has illustrated it; nor yet is it clear
that the difference between the correspondence which
he has discerned and that which Swedenborg claims to
have had revealed to him in the interpretation of the
Bible is other than a difference in degree. May not

every truth of which we find confirmation or illumination from nature, be a correspondence adapted to our plane of intelligence and spiritual evolution? If we can learn modesty from the fringed gentian, faith from the skylark, patience from the maturing processes of vegetation, trust from the succession of the seasons, are we not mastering the alphabet of our Creator, are we not recognizing the correspondence between His thought and the language in which He has sought to make that thought intelligible to us?

"Wisdom," says the learned and pious Hooker in his "Laws of Ecclesiastical Polity," "hath diversely imparted her treasures unto the world. As her ways are of sundry kinds, so her manner of teaching is not one and the same. Some things she openeth by the sacred book of Scripture; some things by the glorious works of nature; with some things she inspireth them from above by spiritual influence; in some things she leadeth and traineth only by worldly experience and practice. We may not so in any one special kind admire her, that we disgrace her in any other; but let all her ways be according unto their place and degree adored."

It has been objected by the literalists that the Holy Scriptures, to be a perfect rule of faith, must be so clear in necessary things as to require no interpretation; that it cannot be a rule or measure where it is obscure, and, therefore, deeper and more interior meanings than those *primæ impressionis* would be inconsistent with a perfect rule of faith. If this be so, why was an interval of several centuries allowed to elapse between the appearance of the Old Testament and the

New? Why was the Old Testament written in tongues which probably not a single one of the disciples of Christ could understand? Why were all the books of the Bible written down in what for centuries have ceased to be living languages, and most of them by men whose names and connexion with the Word have long since passed into oblivion? Upon this theory our Bible could not be a rule of faith to any who do not thoroughly understand the Hebrew, Coptic, Aramaic or Syrian, and Greek tongues, a restriction which has only to be stated to show its absurdity. Why do adults see more in the Word than children; the devout more than the worldly minded; and why does every devout person see new significance in its pages every time he reads them? Nay! Why has our phenomenal world so many mysteries? Why did we have to wait until the Word became ancient literature before we learned that the earth revolved around the sun instead of the reverse; before the waters of the ocean were rendered habitable by the discovery of the compass; before electricity was made the handmaid of civilization? Why does the great book of nature continue to reveal to us secrets no less surprising than any that it has ever previously yielded? Surely we have no more reason for expecting to know all the truths which God has written in His Word at one time or indeed in all time than we have to know at once all the secrets of His mighty works which constitute our earthly environment.

Why do we not judge our fellow man alone by what he says or by his appearance, instead of searching for the motives which animate him? Why do we not talk to our children as we talk to adults? If a ship-builder wished to convey to a child or a ploughman some notion of an ocean steamer, he would not repeat to him his calculations of the strength and quantity of materials, nor his estimates of required power and the means to be employed in securing it. Had we occasion to explain to an illiterate man the ebb and flow of the tides, we should not begin with Newton's famous demonstration. No one's first step in the study of any natural science would be likely to learn anything whatever of the science itself. We could never become astronomers without a knowledge of arithmetic, and yet one may become an expert arithmetician without adding an iota to his knowledge of the heavenly bodies.

There is no more reason why we should comprehend the entire significance of God's Word at sight when uttered in written tongues than when uttered in the language of nature. It seems to be quite as reasonable to insist that man should know at once, even at his birth, all of the phenomenal world that the sciences have been gradually disclosing to us or can ever disclose, or that we will ever need to know, as that he should know at sight all of the spiritual world which the Bible purports to teach. As I have already observed, a message from the Infinite God had to be adapted to every possible stage of spiritual development. It is impossible to conceive of His restricting His light to any nation, tribe, class, age or condition of men. Like the light of the natural sun, it dawns gradually, and the day is half spent before it is diffused with meridian affluence.

It necessarily follows that such a communication does not, and cannot, mean the same thing precisely to any two persons, nor can it mean the same thing to any

103

one person at two successive perusals. Its lessons expand or contract like the pupil of the eye in proportion to the amount of light thrown upon them, and the light will always be supplied and increased so far and so fast, and only so far and so fast, as we carry the lessons of the Word into our lives, for it is only thus and then it becomes light to us. We may safely count upon understanding just so much of the spiritual or interior meaning of the Word as we are prepared to make good use of. More light than that is mercifully withheld, lest we profane it and become blinded forever to the sacred truths it was designed to reveal, as we would be blinded by the rays of sun if their brilliance were not partially obscured by a planetary atmosphere. If our gospel is veiled, said Paul, it is veiled in them that are perishing, in whom the God of this world hath blinded the minds of the unbelieving, that the light of the gospel of the glory of Christ, who is the image of God, should not dawn upon them. * There is no imaginable limit to the heights and depths of the spiritual truths of the Word, for they are infinite. The more the object-glass of the telescope is enlarged, the more extensive the horizon it sweeps and the greater the number of stellar worlds it reveals; so the more faithfully we carry into our daily life the precepts of the Bible as they appear to us, the more light will be thrown upon it and the more will its interior and spiritual meaning well up from inexhaustible fountains.

I will only add to this confession made many years ago, that I do not yet know of any book or lights out-

* II Corinthians, iv. 4.

side of Swedenborg and his interpreters which could have solved the difficulties which confronted me in trying to find the proof in its letter, that the "Word was God"; and my difficulties, I am persuaded, were not unlike, nor less formidable than those which thousands, nay hundreds of thousands, are constantly stumbling over in every Christian land. What an insignificant fraction of the so-called Christian population of the world attend any Church, or participate regularly, or at all, in any of the religious exercises prescribed by the Church, except perchance at a funeral or a wedding? How few comparatively have ever read or heard a chapter of the Bible in their lives! Yet nearly every one of this Gentile population that has been invested with the elective franchise, exercises it. He sees an object in voting; he does not see any object in going to Church. The bread of life that is there broken to him is neither palatable nor satisfying. What means the rapid spread of rationalism throughout the world in these latter days? Whence the enthusiasm for the evolutionary and revolutionary doctrines of Darwin and Huxley and their disciples? Whence the distinction so frequently made even by the clergy between the Old and the New Testament? Whence the increasing skepticism in regard to the Divinity of Christ? Whence the schisms which are rending some denominations, and the dogmatic fatuities which are employed to buttress others? Is it not because theology has not kept up with the thought and spiritual growth of the world? Is it not because the clergy continue to read and interpret the Bible much as they read and interpret any new book just damp from the press, with only the dullest kind of a suspicion of the depths of wisdom it enfolds? Had not Tennyson but too much authority for saying that in the present condition of the Church,

> "There is more faith in honest doubt,
> Believe me, than in half the creeds?"

IX.

I OUGHT not to close this narrative without referring to another incident growing out of my St. Thomas adventures, that I look back upon with great satisfaction for many reasons, not the least important of which was the additional evidence it furnished that in all this West Indian excursion a wiser than I was directing my steps; that I was even then all unconsciously fulfilling the prediction of the prophet, "I will bring you into the wilderness, and there will I plead with you face to face."*

Just before sailing for Hayti, I received some letters of introduction from Mr. B. C. Clark, of Boston, who held the commission of Consul from the Haytian Government for that city. I was not personally known to Mr. Clark, but he was doubtless prompted to this courtesy by Mr. Simones, an agent of the Haytian Government, residing in New York, whom I had consulted about my trip to his country. Among these letters was one to Mr. B. P. Hunt, a merchant at Port au Prince. On our arrival at that port and before we had moored, an elderly gentleman came out to us in a boat, and after briefly saluting the captain, was presented to me. He

* Ezekiel xx. 35.

gave his name as Mr. Hunt; said that Mr. Clark had advised him of my contemplated visit to the island, and if he could be of any service to me during my stay there he wished to place himself at my disposal. I thanked him, handed him my letter of introduction, and after a brief conversation—it was then near sunset—he asked me where I proposed to take my lodgings in Port au Prince. I said I did not yet know, that I should remain on board until morning, and then go on shore and look up the best quarters I could find in the town. He said promptly that that would not do, that it was as much as my life was worth to sleep on the vessel in that harbor until morning; he added that there was not a hotel or boarding house in Port au Prince that I would be content to pass a night in, and that I must go home with him. After satisfying myself that it would be imprudent to decline Mr. Hunt's hospitality, I accompanied him to his quarters, where I remained during my sojourn at Port au Prince, every successive hour of which he made me feel more and more grateful for the circumstances which had inspired him to invite me.

In due time it transpired that Mr. Hunt was a graduate of Harvard College, in the same class with Ralph Waldo Emerson, of whom he had many interesting things to tell me; that without any literary pretensions, he was a man of varied and extensive reading; that he knew more about Hayti, its public men and people, and the books written by or about them, than any one else I ever met there or elsewhere; more, probably, than any other man then living, and with an admirable faculty of communicating his information in conversation. He was a native of Massachusetts, and seemed eminently qualified in every way for a successful career in his native land. For reasons which I never ventured to enquire into, but which I had some reason to suspect had their origin in domestic troubles of some kind, he went out to Hayti, travelled over the island for a year or two, and finally contracted a partnership in a commercial house in Port au Prince, where he had been reasonably prosperous for some thirteen years previous to my making his acquaintance. Aside from the gratitude which I owed him for taking me into his house, without which I probably would have been in the cemetery with most of my recent shipmates within a week after my arrival, I acquired a sincere esteem for the man, an esteem which I think was cordially reciprocated. Mr. Hunt had pretty decided opinions upon most of the great problems of life, and was tolerably familiar, much more than I was then, with what the most eminent writers had written about them. I found his religious opinions, however, even more unsettled if possible than mine. He was a rationalist, without much faith in any future state of existence or in the Divine origin of the Word. He had a well-stocked library of books, with the contents of which he was quite familiar. When I returned to New York, I felt moved to send him an account of the revolution some of my opinions had undergone since we parted, and the circumstances which led to it. I also sent him with some other books, two or three volumes of Swedenborg which I recommended to his notice. In the course of a few weeks I received from him a letter in which he thus alluded to my envoi:

MY DEAR MR. BIGELOW:

I have received your letters of March 14 and 23, with *Evening Post, Swedenborg, Humboldt, Colonial Sal Trade, 7th Census, Medicine Chest* and *Homœopathic Physician, Magazines* and *Riding Whip,* for all of which accept my most sincere thanks, and most particularly for Swedenborg. He seems to have established a "raw" in your mind which I little expected, and I little expected it because in some casual conversation we had about ghosts and the "supernatural" so called, which is perhaps only the natural unexplored, I found you an unbeliever. Swedenborg is not entirely a new acquaintance. About eighteen years ago I had his *Heaven and Hell* and *Apocalypse Revealed* in a former collection of books, and they then made a strong impression on my mind which the cares of the world and the deceitfulness of trying to get "riches" have not wholly effaced, and which your kindness has enabled me to renew. On Sunday last when I got these books I read them, and have been looking into them by snatches ever since, if not with pleasure at least with great interest, for now, as earlier in life, they disturb me. I have not time to say the tithe of what I have to say of this matter, but during these eighteen years, I have considered Swedenborg the father of all those who, in modern times (since Jesus and the prophets) have been able to see spirits, who have given us glimpses (very imperfect) of the spiritual world, and who, in short, have been, and now are, gifted with second sight, animal magnetism and cognate phenomena. I never sought the acquaintance of a Swedenborgian, but when I have casually met them, to the number of half a dozen at long intervals—scholars, ladies, seamstresses, shoemakers, apprentices—I have left their conversation with the impression that I have been talking to a person pure, elevated, spiritual, and in certain departments of the mind, tho' not strong, highly intellectual. In 1841 I asked James Faxon, a shoemaker apprentice in Boston, what was the difference between a good man religious and a good man not religious. He said "Great. The one is good from love of God, the other from love of himself," and he sent me away sorrowful, like the lawyer in the Bible.

In the course of the following year Mr. Hunt's health, always delicate, compelled him to return to the United States to secure the benefit of a higher grade of medical advice than was accessible in Hayti. He took up his residence in Philadelphia.

Knowing how completely he was engrossed by his business when I left him, how little there was in his environment to stimulate such a curiosity as the writings of Swedenborg were likely to satisfy, and the many prejudices which any book that takes the Divine origin and plenary inspiration of the Bible as its point of departure, has to contend with in trying to penetrate the mind of an agnostic of his age and temperament, I was not surprised, though disappointed, by the tone of his letter; nor was I surprised, though disappointed, at hearing nothing more from him about Swedenborg for many years.

In the spring of 1864 I was equally surprised and proportionately gratified by the receipt of a letter from him, most of which was consecrated to Swedenborg and revealed the changes in his views, which can be best described in his own language.

PHILADELPHIA, March 18, 1864.

MY DEAR MR. BIGELOW:

* * * Since these small matters have made it necessary for me to trouble you with this letter, I cannot omit the opportunity of mentioning another and quite different subject.

You may remember that ten years ago this month you sent me at Port au Prince some volumes of the works of Swedenborg, accompanied by a letter which at the time I thought rather remarkable. The volumes in question were *The True Christian Religion, Heaven and Hell,* and *Documents Relating to the Life of Swedenborg.* I looked into those books at the time they were received and later, with awakened curiosity (for earlier in life I had seen them), and sometimes with a more direct interest, but only at intervals, and these often long. The impression these readings made seemed to remain, however, for invariably, during the last three or four years, whenever I have thought of a future state, I have found myself looking at it from Swedenborg's point of view. This winter my chronic complaint, co-operating with choice, has kept me at home a great deal, and after reading in this and that direction for some time I, without any fixed purpose of doing so at the commencement, took up these books, and one after another went carefully through them. There are some things in them which I have not been fully able to appropriate. I do not find a satisfactory account of foreknowledge in its bearing on foreordination, and the persons whose condition in the spiritual world is described are too strictly confined to the theological class. But on the whole, the premise once granted that Swedenborg was the appointed servant of the Lord, the entire system presents the most logical, rational and natural account of man's spiritual nature

111

and future life which I have any knowledge of. In fact it is the only theology which has ever at all commended itself to my acceptance. Besides, the personal character and life of the man have great weight with me as collateral evidence of the truth. Swedenborg did not, like all other, even good founders of sects, Wesley included, seek personal power. He never thought of being at the head of a new organization. He did not seek to make proselytes. He contented himself with simply placing on record the revelations he had been commanded to make, and left it to the Lord to establish His visible Church in His own way and time. He nevertheless speaks as one having authority, and does not argue or beg the question, and this I like, for I am weary of conjecture. I have no value for cases made out by construction. I am seeking for more of his works, and must find out whether Dr. Bush's lectures were ever published except in the *Evening Post*. Meantime I must thank you anew for these volumes, which it has taken me ten years to find the full value of. "Good seed, it seems, will keep."

Some years before this letter was written Mr. Hunt had retired from the commercial house with which he had been connected, and the remainder of his life was consecrated pretty faithfully to his Master's business. He interested himself especially in the people of African descent whom the war had rendered homeless and destitute, and in collecting the children of colored soldiers, orphans especially, into schools. His charity took this direction partly because these people seemed at the time most in need of assistance, protection and instruction, and partly because he had acquired during his long residence in Hayti an interest and respect for the race

which it rarely enjoys in countries where it occupies a
servile position. In 1867 he wrote me a letter from
which I take a single paragraph to show how closely
the Church was associated in his mind with his charities,
and how entirely he had come to regard life as a pre-
cious opportunity which it pained him to see any one
neglect.

1724 FRANKFORD ROAD, PHIL., June 17, 1867.
MY DEAR FRIEND:
This is a country in which all social and govern-
mental experiments that have not been tried on the
other hemisphere, or which have been tried badly,
are to have a fair field; and the late war was the clean-
ing process to get this field ready. Are you ready to
go into it? For, if the New Church is the True
Church, as I firmly believe, it must be made manifest
by able, practical men of the world, who earnestly
carry their faith into practice. *

X

IN looking back over the series of incidents culmin-
ating in the restoration of my faith in the Word, which
I have roughly outlined, how can I hesitate to believe
that I was led—should I not say driven—every step by
the Master? Why did I go to Hayti at all, when there
were so many other places more interesting to visit and

* Mr. Hunt bequeathed that portion of his library which related to the history and vicissitudes of the West India Islands,
and especially of their African population—some 700 volumes—
besides a valuable collection of MS. notes and charts, to the
Boston Public Library.

more accessible, that I had never seen? Why was Mr. Clark, whom I did not know, inspired to give me a letter of introduction to Mr. Hunt, of whom I had never heard? Why did the fever drive me on to another place I had no curiosity to see, and which I omitted no effort to avoid; and why did I happen there just when the disabled French steamer bound for New York and the cholera left me no alternative but to remain two or three weeks instead of as many hours? Why was Mr. Kjerulff the only guest at the hotel with whom I could enter into any social relations? Why did I stumble upon a chapter in the Bible in a morning's reading that provoked me to reveal my agnosticism to this comparative stranger? Why had I been for nearly two months separated from all business cares and preoccupations, and even from books and newspapers, my mind meantime lying fallow, until it had grown hungry and thirsty for something to feed upon, before Mr. Kjerulff placed Swedenborg's books into my hand? Why were we to be fellow-passengers and dependent upon each other exclusively for society for most of the succeeding month? Why, I ask, all these incidents, none of which would have occurred to me if I could have had my own way, unless it was necessary to make me lie down to sleep like Jacob, upon a pillow of stone, that when I should awake I might be ready to exclaim: "Surely the Lord is in this place and I did not know it." Any one of the incidents from the time I left New York, not to speak of those which decided me to go, failing, and I was constantly struggling to make them fail, I might still be without the Bible, if not without a God, in the world. What an unexpected significance my experience has given to the words of the prophet, "It is not in man to direct his way, nor in man that walketh to direct his steps."

> I waited patiently for the Lord;
> And He inclined unto me and heard my cry.
> He brought me up also out of a horrible pit, out of the miry clay,
> And set my feet upon a rock, and established my goings.
> And He hath put a new song in my mouth, even praise unto our God.
>
> *—Psalm xl.* 1-3.

APPENDIX.

A

Miss Rose Kjerulff's letter:

MANITOU, COLORADO, December 18, '95.

DEAR MR. BIGELOW:

The little book you so kindly sent me gives me much pleasure. Of all I have seen written about our Swedenborg, your estimate of him is the most satisfactory. Such a book would be of immense use could it be generally known, but I believe it is not published for the public. Certainly yours was a wonderful experience in our Islands, indeed Providential.

There are some friends of mine in the East whom I would like to have read it, but I prize this copy that you sent me too highly to part with it. One of these friends resides in New York City, whom possibly you may have met. She is of a strictly Presbyterian family, but I believe has joined our New Church Society in 35th Street. She told me she could not accept the cruel doctrines of the old Church. I think hers one of the most spiritual minds I have known.

My father went to heaven in 1874—he was in his 80th year. He was most happy when he knew he was to go, and his spiritual or internal sight was open to behold the other world. One of my sisters who died in Boston in 1868 and a favorite aunt were present with him three days before he went, and they told him that he would be with them in three days. He told the family of this but it was hard to believe, as he did not seem so ill, and the Doctor declared he would be well next day. However, my sister insisted on staying all night with him when she knew my father had said exactly when he was to go, which happened exactly as indicated. Of course they would not tell that Danish doctor how my father knew he was to go just at that hour. I was in New York at the time and only knew of the circumstances on my return home a few months later. My father was more than ever convinced in his last days of the truth of Swedenborg's revelations, and he went joyously to the next world. He was a most spiritual man and did much good while he lived. He had settled in St. Croix the last years of his life, being fond of that Island. I was residing there until the Negro Insurrection in 1878, when my beautiful home there was utterly destroyed, as was the best portion of the estates, and I had to return to this country to my sister and brother-in-law, Commodore Spicer, who then was in command of the Boston Navy Yard. My brother then died intestate, all I possessed in his hands, and then our Dealing Court (Chancery) took everything and gave us nothing, as is the custom in those Colonies for absentees. My youngest sister who had been in Europe a number of years saved enough so that we can exist up in these mountains in seclusion and quiet, which we prefer to a fashionable life. You know something of our West India habits; now we have learned to wait on ourselves, I think we are the happier for it. My nephew George Butler (whose father you were so good to save from consumption in 1868) is now on Government work of irrigation for the Indian Reservation in Arizona, has done masterful work in Montana and will be a useful man to his country. He has great faculty, he was a most wonderful child. We are ever most grateful for your great kindness in helping us as you did when I appealed to you on my arrival from Havana when his mother went to her home in heaven. I trust not to have wearied you with this long letter.

With much esteem I remain,

Sincerely yours,
Rose Kjerulff.

B.

Chronological List of Swedenborg's Principal Theological Works, Translated into English:

Arcana Cœlestia, 1747-1758.

Heaven and Hell, 1757, 1758.

The White Horse, 1757, 1758.

The New Jerusalem and Its Heavenly Doctrines, 1757, 1758.

The Earths in the Universe, 1756, 1758.

The Last Judgment, 1757, 1758.

The Apocalypse Explained, 1757-1759.

Summary Exposition of the Prophets and Psalms, 1759, 1760.

The Doctrine of the New Jerusalem Respecting the Lord, 1761-1763.

The Doctrine of the New Jerusalem Concerning the Sacred Scriptures, 1761-1763.

The Doctrine of Life for the New Jerusalem, 1761-1763.

The Doctrine of Faith of the New Jerusalem, 1761-1763.

Continuation of the Last Judgment, 1763.

The Divine Love and Wisdom, 1763, 1764.

The Divine Providence, 1763, 1764.

The Doctrine of Charity, 1764.

Apocalypse Revealed, 1764-1766.

Conjugial Love, 1767, 1768.

Brief Exposition of the Doctrines of the New Church, 1768, 1769.

Intercourse of the Soul and the Body, 1769.

The True Christian Religion, 1769-1771.

The Coronis, 1771.